Before & After
BATHROOM
MAKEOVERS

By Christine E. Barnes and the Editors of Sunset Books

MENLO PARK, CALIFORNIA

Sunset Books

VICE PRESIDENT, GENERAL MANAGER: Richard A. Smeby

VICE PRESIDENT, EDITORIAL DIRECTOR: Bob Doyle

PRODUCTION DIRECTOR: Lory Day

DIRECTOR OF OPERATIONS: Rosann Sutherland

MARKETING MANAGER: Linda Barker

ART DIRECTOR: Vasken Guiragossian

SPECIAL SALES: Brad Moses

Staff for This Book

MANAGING EDITOR: Sally W. Smith

ART DIRECTOR: Vasken Guiragossian

COPY EDITOR: Barbara Braasch

PRINCIPAL PHOTOGRAPHER: Margot Hartford

PHOTO DIRECTOR/STYLIST: Cynthia Del Fava

ASSISTANT STYLIST: Laura Del Fava

DESIGN CONSULTANT: Annette M. Starkey, CKB, CBD,
    Living Environment Design

ILLUSTRATOR: Beverley Bozarth Colgan

PAGE PRODUCTION: Linda M. Bouchard, Susan Paris

PREPRESS COORDINATOR: Eligio Hernandez

PROOFREADER: Mary Roybal

INDEXER: Nanette Cardon

10 9 8 7 6 5 4 3 2 1
First printing June 2006. Copyright © 2006, Sunset
Publishing Corporation, Menlo Park, CA 94025.
First edition. All rights reserved, including the right
of reproduction in whole or in part in any form.

ISBN-13: 978-0-376-01332-3
ISBN-10: 0-376-01332-X
Library of Congress Control Number: 2006921541
Printed in the United States of America.

For additional copies of *Before & After Bathroom
Makeovers* or any other Sunset book, visit us at
www.sunsetbooks.com or call 1-800-526-5111.

Photography Credits

Cover: Sharon Risedorph Photography (see pages
134–135). Cover design by Vasken Guiragossian.
Page 1: Margot Hartford.
Above: Jamie Hadley.
Opposite, left and top right: Margot Hartford;
bottom right: Ken Gutmaker.
Page 4, top center: Heather Reid. Other images on
pages 4–5: Margot Hartford.

Abbreviations: The following abbreviations are used in the floor plans
shown throughout this book.

B	Bench	L	Laundry
BDR	Bedroom	MBDR	Master bedroom
BI	Bidet	O	Office
CB	Cabinet	S	Sink
CL	Closet	SH	Shower
CN	Control	SHD	Showerhead
D	Dryer	T	Tub
DR	Dining room	T/SH	Tub/shower
GB	Grab bar	W	Washer
HH	Hand-held sprayer	WH	Water heater
IGB	Integral grab bar		

Bathing Beauties

The busier our lives become, the more we look to the bathroom as a personal sanctuary, a spot to refresh and unwind, a place of beauty. It's no wonder we dream of transforming our ho-hum bathrooms into something spectacular.

You can stop dreaming and start planning that new bathroom now, using the before-and-after makeovers on the following pages as your inspiration. You're likely to see (and chuckle at) aspects of your own bath in the "before" photos. In dazzling contrast, the "after" baths illustrate the fundamentals of good design—smart layout, hard-working surfaces, and efficient fittings, to name a few. To add to your arsenal of ideas, plentiful examples showcase up-to-date trends and materials such as undermount sinks, spalike shower fixtures, and slate countertops. Most baths include easy-to-read floor plans that tell at a glance how the space changed; some offer color palettes to help you achieve the look you see.

In addition to the individual bath stories, Special Features focus on choosing bath essentials—sinks, tubs, flooring, and storage. Other features show compartmentalized plans designed for maximum privacy and multiple uses, as well as "wet rooms," where traditional boundaries dissolve into one free-flowing space. Floor plans illustrating the elements of Universal Design provide ideas for making your bath accessible to all.

Far more than just a place to wash up, today's bath calls for practical planning—and a dash of creativity—to transform it into a versatile, comfortable space. Ready to embark on your own bathroom makeover? Let the before-and-after stories shown here inspire and guide you to success.

Contents

SPECIAL FEATURES

The shower took up the **Before** ▶

biggest chunk of space in this dark bath, which was added years after the house was built. The wall between the shower and toilet prevented the lone window from sharing its light with the rest of the room.

Open, airy, and suffused **After** ▶

with natural light, the new room retains its identity as a separate space. Glass partitions above the 7-foot interior walls allow light to spill from the bedroom into the **SLATE-CLAD BATH.** The repeated use of the stone—on the walls, floor, and vanity—endows the surfaces with a sense of simplicity and continuity.

◀ **A double thickness of slate,** laminated to create one weighty slab, makes this wall-mounted vanity all the more striking. Once the homeowner saw the dance of light through the glass bowl and onto the floor, plans for a base cabinet were scrapped.

Floor plans: Seemingly dropped into one corner of the bedroom, the old bath never felt like an integrated part of a plan. The new bath picks up square footage from an existing closet; moving the doorway made the space more usable. A frameless shower door across the width of the room guarantees an uninterrupted visual flow.

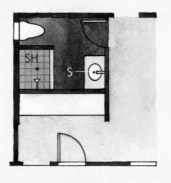

BEFORE   AFTER

◄ **After** | The new bathroom suite, dubbed **"THE BUBBLE BATH"** by its designers, charms guests with translucent trompe l'oeil bubbles painted on a backdrop of soapstone-colored Venetian plaster. (Available at larger paint stores, this popular material is durable and lustrous—but time-consuming to apply.) White Thassos marble tops the Empire vanity and the tub deck.

▲ **The latest amenities** in the tub-shower include a thermal-balance shower system that ensures even water temperature, regardless of water use in other rooms; a tempered-glass shower screen opens out for easy cleaning. On the adjacent wall, the mural continues unimpeded across a blind closet door with a concealed latch and pull.

◄ **A mosaic inlay** of overlapping circles decorates the subway-tile floor; both types of tile are honed Thassos marble.

▲ **Before** | The charm of period tile and glass block could not compensate for the cramped quarters of this master bathroom. A closet belonging to an adjoining bedroom jutted into the space, making the bath seem even smaller.

To achieve | **After** ▶ the spacious, **AIRY RETREAT** desired by the homeowners, the architect and contractor pushed out the wall behind the tub, angled the ceiling, and added garden-view windows. The fitted vanity occupies part of the former closet, leaving the central area of the bath open.

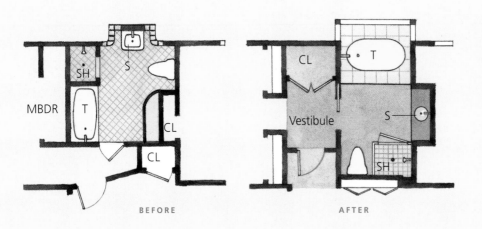

BEFORE   AFTER

Floor plans: In the original plan, an angled doorway into the master suite was awkward and abrupt. Now, a recessed entry leads to a vestibule that opens into the master bedroom on one side and the bath on the other.

▲ **A maple vanity** with stainless steel counter, translucent glass vessel sink, and exposed shelves is the epitome of simplicity. Due to limited wall space, the towel bar is mounted on the shower door.

◄ **Viewed from the bedroom** through the vestibule, the bath is both calm and contemporary. A pocket door with translucent glass can be closed for privacy.

◀ **Before** An open master bath, with its step up to the tub, never felt cozy or comfortable to the homeowners. For privacy's sake, they chose to preserve the glass-block window overlooking a deck.

A gently **After** ▶ arched soffit downplays the existing window and helps create an air of **GRACEFUL INTIMACY** in the remodeled space. Neutral hues and varied textures abound—in the cherrywood cabinetry, concrete countertop, glass-tile backsplash, and limestone-tile floor. A lower threshold makes the undermount tub safer as well as more inviting.

Practicality was part of the plan: The shower curtain hides neatly behind the soffit.

A pony wall between the tub and vanity enhances the sense of enclosure.

With its ditsy wallpaper and **Before** ▶

dingy tile, the guest bath in this century-old home had long shown its age. The family elected to replace a rarely used cast-iron tub with a shower enclosure, but the recently installed pedestal sink segued nicely into their new scheme.

Brand-new **After** ▶

components and a fresh color palette work their magic, reinventing the once dismal space into a bath to boast about. Beadboard paneling showcases a host of **OLD-FASHIONED ACCOUTREMENTS:** a taller, more graceful toilet; brushed-nickel hardware; white ceramic tile; and a vintage-style mirror.

◀ **A 10-inch space** between the top of the shower enclosure and the ceiling improves ventilation and minimizes the "stall" feeling. A chrome-finish, single-control faucet and wall-mounted showerhead keep things simple.

▶ **Plantation shutters** spruce up the storage cabinet and add an architectural element to the scheme.

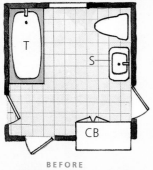

BEFORE

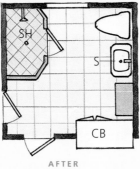

AFTER

Floor plans: An existing floor-to-ceiling cabinet with deep shelving provided ample storage, so there was no need to enlarge the room. Eliminating the third door, next to the sink, increased the wall space and enhanced the sense of privacy.

▼ Before | The old master suite included a dressing area and second vanity, but there was barely enough room to turn around in the toilet and shower compartment. Existing 9-foot ceilings were a real plus, however.

With the boundary | After ▶ between bedroom and bath dissolved, light flows freely through these **MASCULINE QUARTERS,** bouncing off limestone tiles and warm wood casework. The design is defined by smooth, sleek styling and an imaginative floor plan. A focal-point wall with built-in storage and display serves as a backdrop for the bed on one side and the bath vanity on the other.

Bathroom continues ▶ ▶

Floor plans: Without increasing the
square footage—thereby containing
cost—the architect reconfigured the
space to make the suite feel larger.
Angling the wall and bed capitalized
on a stunning marina view.

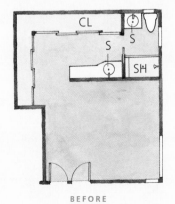

BEFORE

AFTER

◀ **Custom storage** consists of a built-in dresser flanked by a double-door wardrobe and single-door linen closet, all constructed of quarter-sawn maple trimmed in walnut.

▶ **The absence of glass** between the end of the tub and the shower facilitates the visual transition from one space to the other and lets the tub deck serve as a shower bench. For ease of entry, the shower floor is slightly sunken.

▲ **The highly figured marble countertop** features an eased (slightly rounded) edge; just below, recessed hardware preserves the clean lines of the slab cabinet doors.

▶ **A "rug"** composed of tumbled-marble tiles in shades of terra-cotta and sandstone continues the color scheme in bold fashion.

Flooring Options

Moisture resistance, durability, and safety are the chief requirements for bathroom flooring, but good looks matter, too. With the wealth of possibilities, from ancient stone to commercial-grade vinyl, you're guaranteed to find a material that's both handsome and practical.

Resilient Flooring

Commonly made from vinyl or polyurethane, resilient flooring is flexible, tough, and simple to maintain. Vinyl tiles can be mixed to create checkerboard or other patterns; sheet vinyl, which runs up to 12 feet wide, makes a seam-free installation possible in many bathrooms.

Ceramic and Porcelain Tile

Ever-popular ceramic tile is manufactured in glazed and unglazed versions. Fired at relatively low temperatures, unglazed tile is skidproof but must be sealed to prevent water absorption. Glazed ceramic tile has a glasslike material baked onto the surface, giving it a hard, protective shell. Finishes include glossy, matte, and textured; for sure footing, choose matte or textured tile.

▲ A busy bath is the perfect place for easy-care sheet vinyl. This abstract pattern was designed to resemble stained concrete.

Composed of white clay fired at extremely high temperatures, porcelain tile is stronger than ceramic tile and less prone to staining. It is often fabricated to mimic real stone.

Ceramic and porcelain tiles are typically squares from 4 to 24 inches. The larger the tile, the less grout to keep clean; however, smaller tiles with more grout lines provide better traction. To make installation easier, manufacturers premount 1-inch tiles on 12-inch squares of mesh backing.

Stone

For beauty and authenticity, nothing beats natural marble, limestone, and slate. "Honed" marble and limestone are less slippery underfoot than their high-gloss counterparts; slate possesses a natural "tooth" that makes it slip-resistant. Because stone flooring is porous and absorbent, it's essential to apply the appropriate sealer as often as directed.

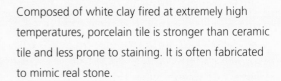

◄ In a bath inspired by nature (see pages 56–59), rustic slate tiles supply earthy color and texture.

▲ Glazed hexagonal ceramic tiles have a textured finish that makes them appropriate for a children's bath; wider grout lines enhance safety.

▲ Classic Carrara marble floor tiles, 24 inches square, combine easily with smaller wall tiles. Marble tiles are typically butted together for a seamless look.

▶ Because limestone is a natural substance, tile coloration can vary widely. In an Italianate guest bath, beveled squares of limestone cover the floor, while subway tiles make up the wainscoting.

▼ Vinyl composition tile, known as VCT, stands up well to water and wear. Here, 12-inch tiles installed on the diagonal create the illusion of a roomier bath (see pages 108–111).

This small bath | **Before** ▶ was considered part of the master suite, but once the homeowners decided to turn the master bedroom into a guest room, plans for the bath changed, too.

The calming colors | **After** ▶ of sand and sea, interpreted in tile, lend a look of **ELEMENTAL ELEGANCE** to the new guest bath. Details make the difference on the distressed-wood cabinet, with its beadboard doors and irregular profile. A metallic-painted mirror frame and a pair of pieced-glass sconces are in sleek contrast to the textured tile surfaces.

◀ **An open shower** is outfitted with a chrome rainfall shower-head and single-handle control. Twelve- and 4-inch travertine tiles cover the shower walls and floor.

▼ **Mosaic glass tiles** on the backsplash (and the shower walls) contrast with the warm travertine in both color and scale.

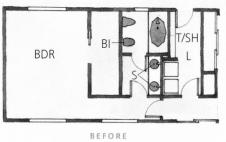

BEFORE

AFTER

Floor plans: For its new role as guest bath, a one-sink vanity suffices. A "wet room" housing the shower and toilet opens to a pool through a new exterior door.

23

▲ Before | A small

bath in a 1960s home had two entrances but no direct access from the bedroom; dueling doors only added to the inconvenience.

Jerusalem limestone, | # After ▶

honed granite, and two types of maple blend beautifully in this spare, **ASIAN-INFLUENCED** design. The open shelf on the granite-topped, curly-maple vanity keeps a light look; a sloping soffit wrapped in plain maple conceals a structural rafter. Two shower heads cater to the homeowners' different preferences.

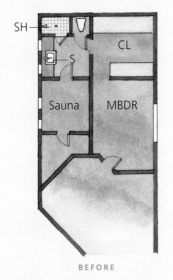

BEFORE

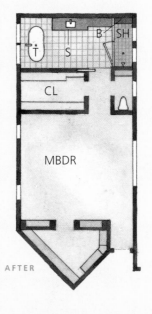

AFTER

Floor plans: The homeowners eliminated the existing sauna in favor of a larger master bath and bedroom and a better-situated closet.

◀ **A maple-frame door** with shoji-screen inserts repeats the neutral color and matte finish of the stone flooring.

▲ **A deep soaking tub,** chosen for its superior heat retention, rests in a maple-and-chrome frame. On the floor, a "brook" of hand-laid river rock meanders through 16-inch limestone tile.

Before
A long run of cabinets in this conventional bath only accentuated its boring layout. As a guest bath, it needed to make a strong impression, as well as provide a sense of privacy.

After
Audacious color and intriguing texture turn a bland space into an **AVANT-GARDE REFUGE,** to the delight and surprise of guests. In contrast to the curves of the sleek mirror and shimmering vanity, Indian slate anchors the scheme with regular pattern and natural texture. An antique Japanese "summer screen" (a seasonal replacement for exterior shoji screens) shields the toilet.

In the spirit of Japanese tansu chests, three stepped windows (the third is over the tub) add form and movement to the design.

Tomato-red walls vibrate with warmth and energy.

Through a wall-mounted vanity made of molded glass, the patterned floor is visible, making the room appear larger; the beechwood towel bar matches decorative shelves above.

27

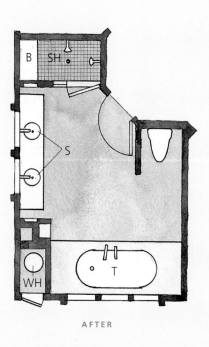

◄Before

Replacing the original metal windows throughout the large home was not an option, so the architect and interior designer devised a plan to work with them. Peach-colored cultured marble on the vanity and gooseneck faucets had long outlasted their era. A wide, angled mirror mounted below the windows only called attention to their presence.

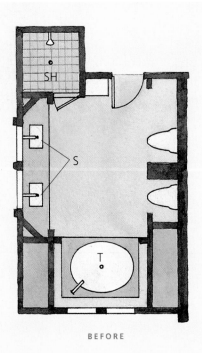

BEFORE

AFTER

Floor plans: The existing bath was generous in size, but two toilets were a waste of space, and the oval soaking tub and square shower enclosure felt undersized for a master bath. The new plan boasts a better-shaped shower and an elegantly proportioned tub.

Bathroom continues ▶ ▶

▼After

Glass, ceramic tile, and stone celebrate the evanescent qualities of light and water in this **ITALIAN-MODERN MASTER BATH.** Bolted to the wall, the glass-topped vanity allows the marble-tile floor to extend underneath for an ethereal, space-enhancing effect. Mirrors installed slightly away from the wall subdue the dark window frames and balance the horizontal countertop.

Color Palette

"Ming" and "spring" green fool the eye into seeing interlocking circles in the floor mosaic; soft white serves as the backdrop. On the tub apron and the walls, ceramic tiles in a hue described as "green veil" carry the monochromatic scheme upward.

▶ **A deep soaking tub** sited below tall windows overlooks a private garden; strands of shell circles hanging on tension rods veil the view. To accommodate a bather (or two) reclining against either end of the tub, the faucet components are installed front and center. A contemporary chandelier from Italy adds formal flair.

▼ **A mosaic-tile border** made up of Thassos marble accentuates the elegantly angled footprint of the room. At the perimeter, between the mosaic border and the tile baseboard, minibrick tiles form narrow bands. Small, rectangular field tiles are set in a two-step, or "twist," pattern.

▶ **Located conveniently between the tub** and the vanity, deep storage cupboards hold everything required and desired in a deluxe master bath. Euro-style hinges (see pages 64–65) keep the working hardware hidden.

Bathroom continues ▶ ▶

▲ **The shower interior** is fitted with a hand-held wand sprayer and a slotted soap basket; on the floor, a variation in the tile pattern sets it apart from the rest of the bath.

▶ **Trim tiles in the wainscoting** repeat the circle motif in the mosaic-tile border underfoot.

▶ **This one-of-a-kind glass counter** with integral sinks began as a layer of smashed white glass, topped by a sheet of clear glass. The two materials were then fused by lengthy firing at high temperatures, producing a reflective surface that is both transparent and opalescent.

▲ **At each end of the vanity,** a built-in medicine cabinet opens by means of a recessed groove at the lower corner; the mirrored interior adds a bit of glamour and surprise.

▶ **A floor-to-ceiling privacy wall** creates a toilet alcove apart from the rest of the room. With its tank concealed behind the wall, the toilet appears to float in space; the flushing mechanism is mounted above, on the wall.

▲ Relaxed Roman shades are topped by matching valances in this sophisticated, symmetrical master bath. Unlined, they afford only daytime privacy when lowered.

▼ The natural colors and textures of flat woven shades complement the lines of a ribbed-glass pocket door in an elegant master bath.

Window Treatments

A comfortable bathroom feels private, and nothing ensures privacy more than well-chosen window treatments. Even when privacy is not a primary concern, the right window treatment can control light, insulate against heat and cold, and complete a bath in style.

Window coverings fall into two broad categories: "soft" and "hard." Treatments may be mounted in either of two ways: within the window frame (inside mount) or on the window frame or the wall itself (outside mount).

Soft Window Treatments

Roman shades, London shades, cloud shades, and curtains have one thing in common that defines them as soft window treatments—fabric.

With their crisp, flat folds, Roman shades look handsome made up in geometric patterns, stripes, and solid-color fabrics; billowy cloud shades and relaxed London shades are better suited to floral or toile prints. Curtains in all lengths—café, apron, or to-the-floor—soften windows and imbue a bath with unexpected elegance. For both daytime and nighttime privacy, choose lined fabric treatments.

Hard Window Treatments

Blinds, cellular shades, roller shades, woven shades, and shutters are termed hard window treatments, although many shades in this category are fabricated from high-tech, moisture-resistant materials that resemble fabric. They're appropriate in tailored or sleek settings, as well as in small baths that lack the space for more voluminous fabric treatments.

Combination Treatments

For both practicality and beauty in the bath, soft and hard window treatments are frequently paired. Valances (short, stationary versions of fabric window treatments) soften hardworking shades and blinds and hide their headings.

Inside-mount Treatments

In tight spaces, with little room on either side of a window, inside-mount treatments are the only option. They're also a good choice for windows with handsome casings. Manufacturers fabricate inside-mount treatments with minimum clearances to maximize privacy and insulation.

Outside-mount Treatments

If space allows, consider installing the treatment on the window frame or the wall. Outside mounts provide superior insulation and privacy and allow you to "stack" the treatment completely off the glass.

▼ Part blind and part sheer fabric, these shades filter light and preserve daytime privacy when the slats are open. With the slats tilted up or down, the treatment blocks light and provides complete privacy.

▲ An architectural element in their own right, plantation shutters with 2-inch louvers offer better ventilation and a clearer view than traditional narrow-louvered shutters.

▶ In an authentic Victorian bath, café curtains with Paris pleats—pinched at the heading, not at the base of the pleats—soften the view while maintaining privacy. Above, a London shade serves as a valance or, when lowered, functions as an additional insulating layer.

◄ Before

The walls in this newly remodeled guest bath were a blank canvas waiting for color. Willow-green ceramic tile on the vanity was an obvious starting point.

Fresh blue and green bathe the

After ►

new space in **COOL, AQUATIC COLOR.** Papered with white tissue and glazed two shades of turquoise, the walls make a bright backdrop for a mosaic mirror and white étagère. Glass tile left over from the mirror trims the shades on the light bar.

▼ **Cut-to-fit pieces** *(left)* of "bullnose" (rounded-edge) tile frame the window casing. Raw-edge squares of fabric stitched between two layers of clear vinyl form the flat curtain panel.
To create a crinkled wall surface *(right),* tissue was applied with wallpaper paste, then wrinkled while the paste was still wet. A matte topcoat sealer protects against moisture.

◄ Before | The large master bath's existing floor, vanity, and shower enclosure were in fine shape, but the tub was too small and the wood window seat too wide.

◄ **After** | Slab *creama marfil* (creamy marble) on the new tub deck and seating area transforms a once-awkward corner into a harmonious **PLACE OF REPOSE.**

A decorative band of *pietra azzurrata,* a type of honed marble, encircles the room.

▲ **Walls painted tidepool blue** act as a cool backdrop for a white-framed mirror and polished-nickel sconces. In the mirror's reflection is a wall-mounted television, with its speaker installed above.

◄ **Cap, mosaic, and liner pieces** of *pietra azzurrata* inject natural color and texture into the refined scheme. The small tile squares are "hand chopped" to give them irregular edges.

Bathroom continues ▶ ▶

▲ **Before** | The existing bath was just too small to be shared by a teenage boy and his younger sister. Access to the backyard was a priority, along with a secondary sink and more storage.

Pâpier-maché fish **After** ▶ that captivated the homeowner were the design catalyst for this imaginative, kid-friendly **AQUARIUM BATH.** The partition between the tub and toilet compartments marks the original exterior wall; the rectangular cutout adds an element of fun and admits welcome light into the combined tub-shower.

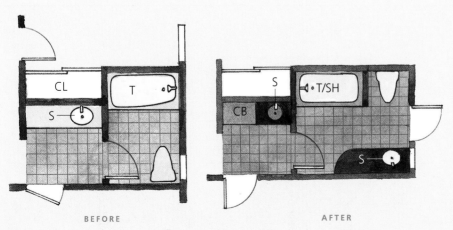

Floor plans: A 3½-foot addition to the side of the house allowed space for a new toilet and vanity with an undermount sink. (The new tub-shower and vessel sink occupy roughly the same spots as in the existing plan.) A door opening into the garden replaces the original window.

BEFORE

AFTER

◀ **Tub and shower fixtures** include, from the top, an adjustable-height sprayer, water-flow controls, a thermal-balance control, a diverter, a Roman tub filler, and an overflow.

▶ **The composite countertop** with integral backsplash extends in a graceful curve beyond the cabinet base, creating a larger surface; the open area below can accommodate a small stool or wastebasket.

▲ **One-of-a-kind, handmade fish tiles** appear to swim in a sea of polished glass. The tile maker and homeowner set the fish first; a professional installer followed with 1-inch glass tiles.

▶ **The vessel sink and storage cabinets** are easily accessed from the nearby hall. Visible in the mirror are the colorful painted-paper fish that started the scheme.

Floor plans: The homeowners were willing to forfeit one of the bedrooms to gain a master bath and walk-in closet. The vestibule is a calm transition zone from one activity area to the other.

BEFORE

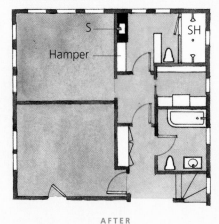

AFTER

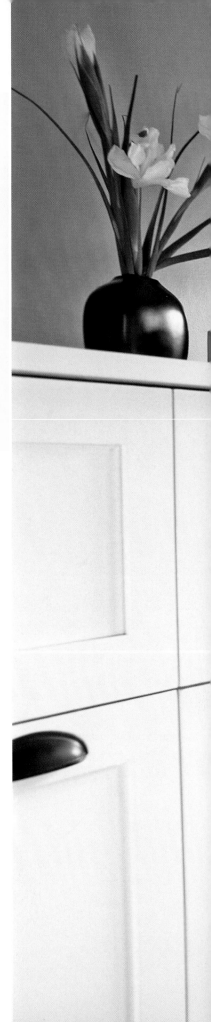

▲ **Before** | With just one bathroom for three bedrooms, access was the issue: from the far bedroom, the bath could be reached only by walking through one of the adjoining rooms. It was, to say the least, a far-from-ideal traffic pattern.

Built in 1913, this classic Prairie- | **After** ▶ style home merited a makeover plan that would stay **TRUE TO TRADITION**—and give the homeowners the efficient, up-to-date master bath they desired. The tall, three-bin clothes hamper combines vintage style with modern practicality; a vanity with an above-counter sink and honed black granite surface packs plenty of storage.

Bathroom continues ▶ ▶

◄ Both a privacy feature and a storage piece, the tall shelving unit separates the toilet and shower area from the vanity and hamper. Every inch is put to use: the lower portion of the unit, covered in cottage board on this side, is open on the other side for additional storage.

▶ Hexagonal mosaic tiles form an eye-catching shower "rug"; for safety's sake, the tiles have a slip-resistant finish. First seen by the home-owner as a small sample in a tile showroom, the pattern was extrapolated by the tile installer to fit the shower floor.

▲ A single French door brings welcome light from the bathroom into the vestibule. Reeded glass panes, installed in alternating directions, preserve privacy in the bath and add a bit of pattern to the simple scheme.

◄ The custom hamper was the brainchild of the homeowners, who wanted a good-looking system for separating and storing laundry. Dirty clothes go through push-flap doors above (just like those found in fast-food-restaurant recep-tacles) and fall into the bins below; liners make it easy to remove the contents and tote them to the laundry room.

"It's all about the choreography of the space. When I reach for my toothbrush, will I get poked by that fabulous door pull I had to have? It's the little things—what goes where—that make the difference in how the bathroom works for you."

Before

A Jack-and-Jill bath configured with a vanity on either side of the tub-and-toilet compartment didn't meet this changing family's needs. Twenty-year-old materials and components were hopelessly dated.

A bold plan for the existing space produced a **VERSATILE FAMILY BATH** that pleases—and works for—everyone. The L-shaped vanity offers plenty of counter space and storage. Above the counter, cubbies can hold items the kids use; higher cabinets keep other objects out of reach.

After

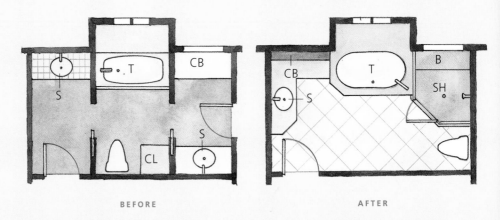

Cherrywood cabinetry is a popular choice for a traditional bath.

Floor plans: Closing off one of the doors to the bathroom made it possible to install a corner shower enclosure at one end of the room and a single-sink vanity at the other. The plan meant the existing windows could stay, a big plus for the budget-minded homeowners.

BEFORE

AFTER

Large limestone tiles in a neutral color "ground" the floor.

▶ **Integral grab bars in the tub** and a bench in the shower are important safety features for a bath used by all ages. (To accommodate shower grab bars down the road, the contractor reinforced the walls.) Magnetized tiles on the tub apron permit easy access to the plumbing.

Marble tiles inject natural color and pronounced pattern into the design.

▲ A freestanding cabinet with drawers and a micro-patterned glass door has an unfitted look suited to a retro-style bath.

Storage Solutions

Efficient, stylish storage is a must in any well-planned bath, and, happily, manufacturers continue to oblige storage-hungry homeowners with an abundance of good-looking, functional options. Although the built-in vanity (see pages 64–65) is still the storage hub in many a bath, other possibilities abound.

Recessed

If your makeover plan includes opening the walls for plumbing or wiring work, why not take advantage of the opportunity to install storage between the studs? Recessed cabinets provide closed storage for oft-used items, while niches and open shelves display bath accessories—all without eating up valuable floor space. A niche set into a shower or tub wall is convenient for holding soap, shampoo, razors, and the like.

Freestanding

In a bath with a pedestal sink or console vanity, you'll need storage for the grooming gear and cleaning supplies normally housed in the base of a built-in vanity. "Unfitted" storage includes new cabinets and shelves designed just for the bath, as well as vintage furniture pieces.

Wall-mounted

Hanging storage can take up the slack in a bath with limited floor space or no below-counter storage. A wall-mounted cabinet makes the most of space next to a sink or above the toilet. (Just be sure the cabinet clears the head of a seated person.) A multiple-hook rack can hold more towels than the typical towel bar; where wall space is limited, install robe hooks.

◄ In this small but sophisticated bath (see page 125), a vintage-style cabinet made of metal and glass houses linens and toiletries. Exposed legs allow light to spill under the piece for an airier effect.

◄ Mounted above the toilet, a cottage cabinet supplies extra storage. Painting the interior and the wood knobs to match the countertop tile (see pages 36–37) gives the piece a custom look.

▲ Upper cabinets with flush-inset doors and drawers utilize space between the countertop and the soffit; glass doors keep the tall cabinets from looking top-heavy.

▲ In a bathroom with a drop-in tub (see pages 92–93), the surrounding walls offer great opportunities for storage. Here, an open-shelving unit features a cornicelike frame with beadboard backing.

▶ Towering cabinets offer serious storage in a spacious bath. The flush-inset, frame-and-panel doors are a blend of traditional and contemporary styles.

▼ Overnight visitors use small comic-strip placards created by the homeowner to identify their towels. The wall-mounted unit includes a mirror, a narrow shelf, and hooks.

▲ Before

Once part of an enclosed porch, this postage-stamp bath had been unusable for years. The adjoining room was "like a second garage," a natural magnet for clutter.

Soothing | After ▶

materials and versatile components imbue the new bath with **SPALIKE SIMPLICITY** and function. Shimmering glass tile on the vanity backsplash continues into the shower for a seamless transition. Travertine tile covers the remaining shower walls and ceiling; on the floor, smaller tile with wider grout lines provides a slip-resistant surface.

Floor plans: The old layout shows just how poorly the space was used previously. Even with an expanded bath and a walk-in closet, the new plan allows room for a generous dressing area.

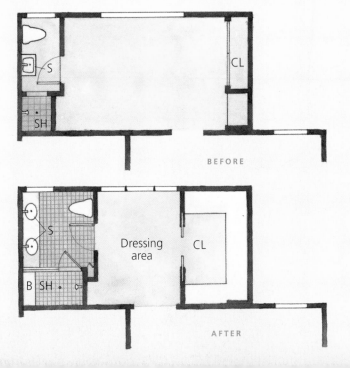

CL

SH

S

BEFORE

S

Dressing area

CL

B SH

AFTER

▼ An adjustable-height, hand-held sprayer mounted near the bench comes in handy for bathing the couple's young son; the wall gauge nearby governs steam from a floor vent. A second set of shower fixtures incorporates a thermal-balance system to maintain water temperature.

▶ A silver-leaf mirror frame blends with satin-nickel downlights and wide-spread vanity faucets. Slab travertine on the counter-top includes a traditional ogee edging.

LESSONS FROM THE HOMEOWNERS

"We really listened to our hearts—for example, we didn't put in a tub because we realized we would never use it. What we got may not have perfect 'resale value,' but it's our dream bath."

◀ Before
"Claustrophobic" and "boring" best described this windowless bath. Located in an active area of the house, just off the home gym and media room, the space was neither fun nor functional.

Wall-to-wall pebble tiles set the stage for **A CLEAN GETAWAY** # After ▼

in this dramatic steam bath. White river rock embedded in green resin makes up the 12-by-12-inch tiles and the slab countertop. In working with the material, the designer observed that light would shine through the resin, a quality he effectively exploited by back-lighting the tile around the mirror.

The steam control is easily adjusted by a seated person.

An undermount sink keeps the countertop sleek.

Green glass pulls accent the tile-encrusted vanity.

▼ **Before** | Unremarkable in every way, the small master bath with stock fixtures begged for a new look. First on the long list of items to go were the cabinets.

The secret ingredients in this recipe | **After** ▶
for renewal? Equal parts **IMAGINATION AND INNOVA- TION.** The homeowners began their bold makeover by fitting a gardener's potting bench with a bar sink and farm-style faucet. Earthy—and unusual—materials and components followed.

Bathroom continues ▶ ▶

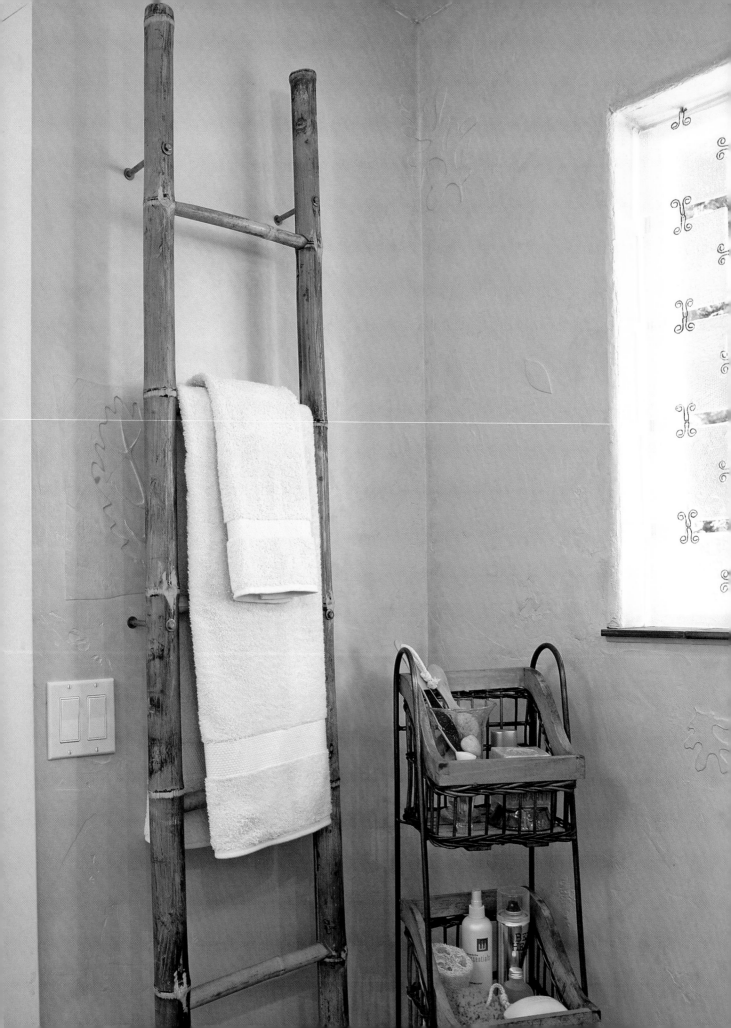

◀ **Bolts installed through the upright pieces** and into the studs turn a bamboo ladder into a towel bar.

▶ **Paint containing lime** "blooms" as it dries on the wall, creating a natural, mottled effect. Here, lime paint brings out bas-relief motifs executed with stencils and joint compound.

▼ **Instead of being recessed** into the wall, this cabinet was bolted to the surface so the mirror could hang in front of the bench.

◀ **Textured tiles made of recycled glass** are linked by copper wires embedded in the glass. The "curtain" obscures an undesirable view.

▲ **A low-voltage track lighting system** acts as both design element and energy saver. A transformer allows the system to operate on 12 volts rather than 120. The satin-nickel rail can be bent by hand.

▲ Before | The existing bath in

this 1935 Monterey Mission home suffered from old age, but the basic layout, which included a built-in vanity near the sink, had stood the test of time.

A healthy | # After ▶

respect for what was there guided the homeowners as they deftly took their bath **FROM PAST TO PRESENT.** Fresh paint, polished-chrome hardware, and a blend of tile and stone come together in a space that boasts brand-new components and plenty of retro charm.

Floor plans: Although the footprint did not change, the room gained precious inches from hall linen closets on either side of the door. What was lost in storage was minimal compared to the benefit of a larger bath.

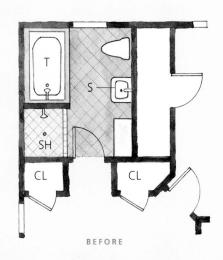

BEFORE

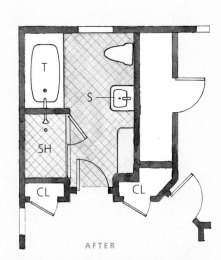

AFTER

A new console sink with gleaming fixtures stays true to the spirit of the original design. Mounted away from the wall, the mirror and attached glass shelf maintain the open effect.

▲ **Tiles from various sources** lend an air of authenticity to the design. Glossy ceramic tiles with a crackle finish flank a decorative border composed of tumbled stone and small, triangular pieces of the floor tile.

▲ **Crackle-finish tile** absorbs some moisture, so the home-owners chose smooth tiles to line the shower enclosure. The right cross-handle controls the flow to the hand-held sprayer; the left governs the showerhead.

▶ **The new recessed tub** only resembles a period piece; a graceful tub filler with cross-handle controls adds old-fashioned appeal.

▼ **The existing vanity** got a simple face-lift with white paint, new knobs, and 5-inch glossy tiles. Darker, matte-finish tiles on the floor measure 4 and 2 inches square.

Color Palette

Although the color scheme might be classified as monochromatic, the hues in the tile palette are myriad and subtle: a mix of greens in the mosaic border, Arts and Crafts green on the floor, lichen green in the shower, and pale, creamy trim atop the white wainscoting.

Vanity Basics

No matter how many family members use a bathroom, the vanity almost always functions as "command central." It holds a sink or two, supplies a surface for a host of everyday items, and typically provides below-counter storage. With so many roles to fill, the vanity merits careful consideration in any makeover plan.

Vanities fall into two broad categories: fitted cabinetry and unfitted, furniture-like pieces.

Fitted Cabinetry

The fitted, or built-in, vanity remains popular because it offers storage in the base, referred to as the "box." There are two types of box construction for fitted vanity cabinets: face-frame and frameless.

Face-frame cabinets have a wood frame attached to the front edges of the box. Doors and drawers fit into the opening or cover part of it, but the frame always shows. The hinges may or may not show.

Frameless cabinets have no frame attached to the face of the box. Open the door and you see the edges of the box itself; close the door and the edges are covered. Hidden hinges (often called "Euro-style" hinges) are attached to the inside.

Doors and drawers differ in the way they fit the cabinets.

Flush-inset doors and drawers close flush with the frame on face-frame cabinets. It's the most expensive style because a precise fit is required.

▲ Frameless cabinets with full-overlay doors and drawers suit sleek, contemporary baths. In this Asian-style scheme, horizontal bamboo panels on the long vanity set a tranquil tone.

▼ A bombé (bowfront) vanity showcases face-frame cabinets with flush-inset doors and drawers. Raised panels impart a subtle dimension, yet when closed the doors and drawers fit flush with the frame openings.

▲ Jerusalem gold limestone, sealed with a color enhancer for a richer effect, rests on the chrome frame of this sleek console vanity. The hammered-nickel basin is cone-shaped to minimize splashing.

▲ A wall-mounted vanity made of glass and mahogany is just the thing in a tiny powder room. The clear glass backsplash, installed over the neutral wall color, takes on a green tinge.

Partial-overlay doors and drawers cover the openings on face-frame cabinets while revealing some of the frame. They are less expensive than flush-inset doors and drawers because there is some "play" in the fit.

Full-overlay doors and drawers cover the box completely on frameless cabinets, with just a bit of space between the doors and drawers for clearance.

Doors and drawers come in two styles: frame-and-panel and slab.

Frame-and-panel doors are by far the more popular. A flat, recessed, or raised panel rests within a door frame made up of two horizontal "rails" and two vertical "stiles."

Slab doors can be solid wood, but they are usually made up of several layers.

Unfitted Options

Unfitted vanities run the gamut, from furniture that has been adapted to accept plumbing to console versions with exposed legs and wall-mounted units without legs. The trade-off for exposed below-counter storage (or no storage) is a lighter feel that's perfect for small or open-plan baths.

◄ A combined vanity–dressing table marries face-frame cabinets and marble countertops. The partial-overlay doors and drawers cover some of the cabinet frame.

► Outfitted with a wide-spread faucet, undermount sink, and marble top, a mahogany table takes on a new purpose as a freestanding vanity.

65

Nothing | **After** ▶ distracts from the **NATURAL SURROUNDINGS** of wood and stone in the new master bath. With elegant ease, slate tiles in varying sizes and grid patterns extend into the shower; a gently vaulted ceiling reinforces the longitudinal continuity of the space. Opposite the fir-and-granite vanity is a laundry center with upper storage.

▲ **Before** | The original bathroom in this 1914 period house was small by today's standards. Fortunately, an adjacent study, once a sleeping porch, gave the architect and home-owners room to maneuver, quite literally, as they formulated a new plan.

Floor plans: Without diminishing the size of the bedrooms, the archi-tect combined and reapportioned the existing bath and study to cre-ate a larger master bath and small guest bath.

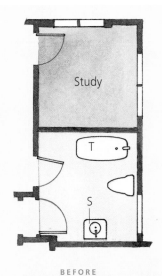

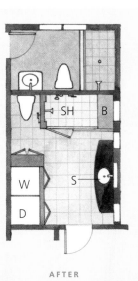

BEFORE

AFTER

◀ **With its gently bowed front,** the vanity echoes the curve of the vaulted ceiling. Face-frame cabinets feature flush-inset doors and drawers, the most precise (and costliest) type of cabinet construction (see pages 64–65).

▶ **Compact and organized** with an eye to efficiency, the built-in laundry center houses the washer and dryer; the fir countertop can be removed if necessary. When closed, the wood-and-glass doors hide the appliances but not the upper cabinetry.

▼ **The 7-foot-high cupboard** located just around the corner from the laundry center has a slim footprint but plenty of storage in the upper cubbies. Squares of mahogany accent the fir frame.

◀ **A tankless water heater** fits compactly behind the lower doors of the cupboard. Water is heated only as it flows through the unit, in contrast to a conventional heater.

▲ **Green granite** with serpentine graining flows the length of the vanity. An undermount sink leaves the handsome surface largely uninterrupted; the wide-spread faucet is copper, as are the shower and bidet fixtures.

In the narrow toilet alcove, a hand-held sprayer and a wall-mounted control take the place of a standard bidet.

▼ **Great design is in the details:** an inward-sloping shower bench makes rising from a seated position easier and safer. Capping the shower dam with the darker granite rather than the lighter slate gives a visual cue that a threshold, although low, is there.

▲ **An electrical receptacle** inside the medicine cabinet helps maintain a clutter-free countertop.

NOTES FROM THE ARCHITECT

"I've become a big fan of slate, in part because it's such an incredible deal. In this bath it struck the perfect balance between the toothy texture of a natural material and a smooth, uniform surface that's friendly to a naked body."

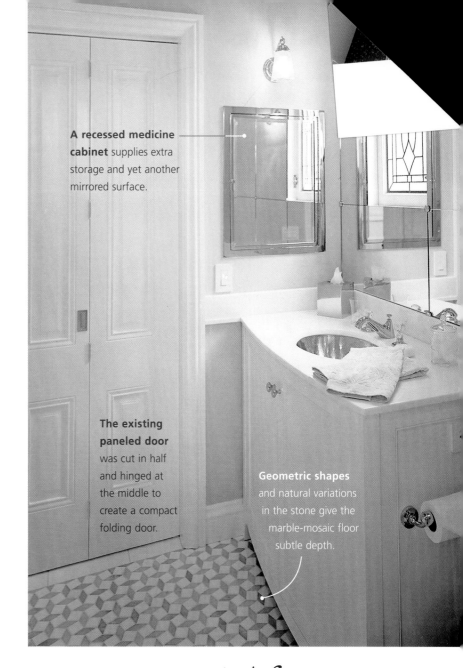

A recessed medicine cabinet supplies extra storage and yet another mirrored surface.

The existing paneled door was cut in half and hinged at the middle to create a compact folding door.

Geometric shapes and natural variations in the stone give the marble-mosaic floor subtle depth.

▲ Before | For a

guest bath, the space was adequate, but as "her" everyday bath, it was uninspiring. The existing leaded-glass window was the only feature to remain.

▼ **Nickel-plated "buttons"** mark the corners where the mirror sections meet. (A metal fabricator cut the buttons in half for the lower and outer edges.) The pounded-nickel sink and crystal handles glisten in the reflected light.

Glamour prevails in this simple, | ## After ▲

sophisticated bath with its pretty palette and

SPARKLING SURFACES. White Thassos marble on the countertop and shower surfaces bounces light, while sections of mirror extending from the backsplash to the ceiling give the appearance of an airier space. A gently bowed vanity is another luxe touch.

▲ Before

Dark wallpaper in the windowless vanity area of this master bath was oppressive, while awkward steps consumed floor space in the tub-shower room.

Quiet colors | # After ▶

plus natural patterns soothe and refresh mind and body in this **SERENE MAKEOVER.** Minimalist wallpaper lightens and visually expands the space; green-and-black granite stands out against white marble tile.

◀ **A walk-in shower** with bench and frameless glass door is by far the homeowners' favorite feature. The new awning window provides natural ventilation; obscuring glass ensures privacy.

◄ Before | Last remodeled decades ago, this tiny bath possessed not a single redeeming feature. For the homeowner/architect, its sorry condition offered the opportunity to relocate the bath and start afresh.

A copper sink rescued from a | After ►

salvage yard finds a new home—and a **NATURAL SYNERGY**—among a medley of warm-toned materials. "I loved the shape of the sink, the look of the metal," the homeowner says, "and I knew a plan for the room would follow."

▼ **Mexican mosaic glass tiles** blend beautifully with the sink's patina. (The homeowner opted not to seal the sink, to preserve its "living finish.") A protective copper strip replaces the usual tile edging on the vanity.

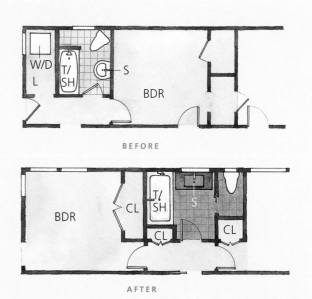

BEFORE

AFTER

Floor plans: Now situated between the two bedrooms, the new, larger bath affords easy access and more privacy for the homeowners and their kids, plus storage closets that open to the hall. (The existing laundry room was moved to another part of the house.)

Mexican "brick" tiles and brass fixtures saturate the room with rich color.

The custom cherrywood vanity, designed by the home-owner/architect, is fitted with glass panels sandblasted in a pattern of tiny squares.

NOTES FROM THE HOMEOWNER/ARCHITECT

"Design for yourself, not for 'the average person.' If you try to please everyone, you'll end up with a room that's mundane—and not really yours."

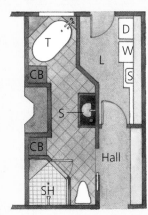

◄Before | The existing guest bath layout was a nightmare for the homeowners, who had to walk through the vanity area and the toilet compartment to get to the laundry room.

Remodeling both | **After ►** rooms yielded a narrower bath, but the designer made up for it with an **ANGULAR FLOOR PLAN** and a design that reflects the homeowners' travels. An Asian-style vanity houses a semirecessed vessel sink, easy for the grandchildren to reach. On the floor is India slate punctuated by small diamonds of black granite.

Bathroom continues ► ►

Floor plans: In the remodeled plan, a new auxiliary hall permits easy access to both bath and laundry room. The angled tub and shower at opposite ends of the room maximize the limited space, as does the pocket-door entry.

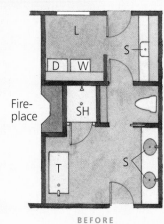

BEFORE

AFTER

◀ **The slate-covered alcove** gives the free-standing tub a cozier feel—and makes cleaning around it much easier. The flat surfaces are ideal for accessories or decorative pieces.

▶ **The walk-in shower** features a grab bar near the bench and an adjustable-height, hand-held sprayer mounted on a shower bar.

▼ **Standard linen cabinets** measuring 21 by 84 inches fit into the spaces on either side of the fireplace box that protrudes from an adjoining room.

▲ **Pewter-finish cabinet hardware** harmonizes with the intricate pattern on the mirror frame (page 77).

▶ **One wall-mounted cross handle** controls water flow to the tub filler, the other to the hand-held sprayer. Above them, a single handle adjusts water temperature.

Wet Rooms

Another term for a wet room—"open shower"—says it all. This design concept makes a bathroom appear larger because there are no doors or walls to demarcate the shower. And though you're showering indoors, a wet room brings an outdoor quality and a feeling of freedom to the experience.

Turning a standard shower into a wet room is not without challenges: The shower pan must be sloped for drainage, and everything within the shower's reach must withstand moisture. When a tub is included in a wet room, it's usually situated near the showerhead to keep water in one part of the room.

If you long for the look of an open shower yet want to control the spray a bit, a narrow, inconspicuous screen of tempered glass or other transparent material near the showerhead can accomplish both objectives.

▲ In this wet room, a low-profile stainless steel sink has a hidden drain (at the back) for a sleek look. Double-jointed kitchen faucets can reach the entire length of the sink, which stretches from one wall to the other.

▶ In the same bath, fiery red opalescent tiles run across the ceiling, down the back wall, and along the floor. The room's side walls are coated with the same waterproof, integral-color plaster used on swimming pools and outdoor show-ers. For simplicity and ease of cleaning, everything, including the toilet and cantilevered sink, hangs from the walls.

▲ White subway tiles and polished-chrome fixtures give this wet room its urban ambience. A goose-neck showerhead and minimalist hand-held sprayer are at once utilitarian and ultracontemporary.

▲ Both tub and shower go behind glass in this practical layout. A central floor drain serves both the wall- and ceiling-mounted showerheads; a rack mounted high on the wall keeps towels dry.

▶ White marble on the walls, floor, and tub surround makes this wet room feel like open territory; warm-toned mosaic tiles play up the shower tower. On the right, a slim glass screen controls splashes.

▼ Without a heavy partition separating the shower from the tub, this wet room feels grander than it is. A glass panel shields the vanity from shower spray; the high window washes the space in daylight yet protects the homeowners' privacy.

▸ Before │ As the only bath in a 1920s bungalow, this small room was woefully inadequate. A separate tub and shower were at the top of the home-owners' must-have list.

Nearly doubled in size, the │ After ▸ new bath offers a clean, contemporary take on traditional **COTTAGE STYLE.** Crisp white cabinetry supports a solid-surface counter-top and integral sinks. Glass pulls and the ceramic tile inspired the fresh color scheme.

Floor plans: The 8-foot addition to the back of the house made room for a fitted layout with two-sink vanity, recessed tub, and corner shower.

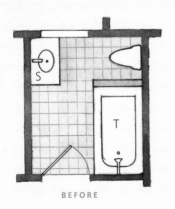

BEFORE

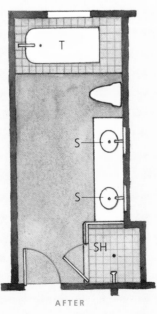

AFTER

Bathroom continues ►►

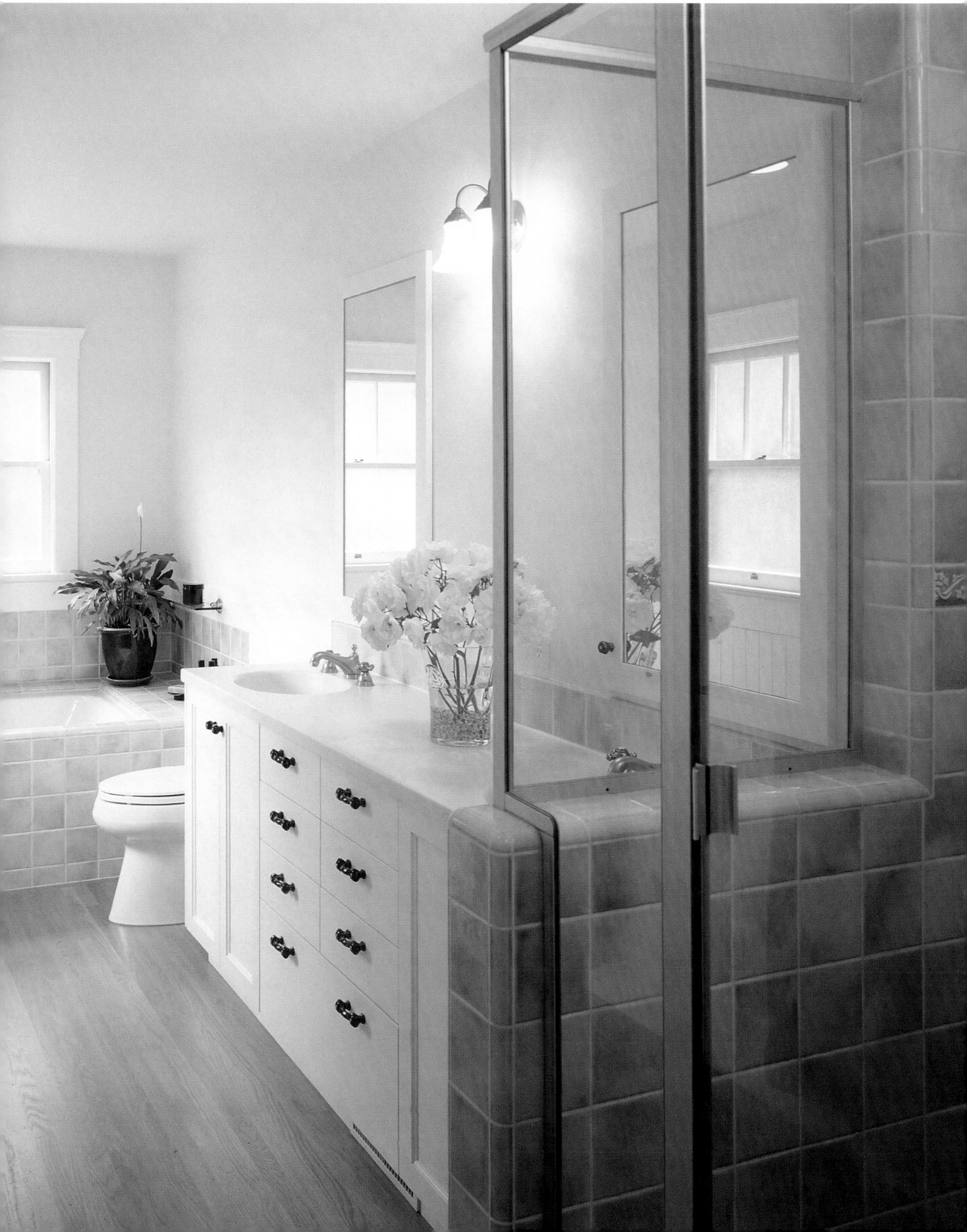

Obscuring glass supplies just enough privacy in windows overlooking a secluded garden.

Three-inch beadboard and 8-inch baseboards look as though they have always been there. A chair rail links the windowsills and paneling.

Red oak flooring blends with the home's existing floors.

◄ **A shallow medicine cabinet** fits neatly between the studs. Ceramic tiles surrounding the tub and lining the shower were carefully arranged to look like clouds in a summer sky.

◀ Before | For the 6-foot-plus teenager who used this bathroom, the standard vanity was too short. In addition, stock components and dated surfaces hardly reflected his budding interest in design.

▼ After | A family vacation to Italy inspired this 14-year-old's vision for his new bath, but budget limitations dictated an economical approach. After

months of bargain hunting at home centers and on the Web (and with assistance from a contractor), the **SLEEK BUT SENSIBLE** dream took shape.

A wall-mounted faucet with polished-chrome finish features a right-angle spout; the lever handle is positioned to the right.

The stainless steel vessel bowl continues the shiny look and adds a sculptural accent.

The reflective countertop is composed of economical black granite tile, 12 inches square.

A new kitchen cabinet from a furniture discount store is 36 inches high, taller than the standard 31-inch bathroom vanity.

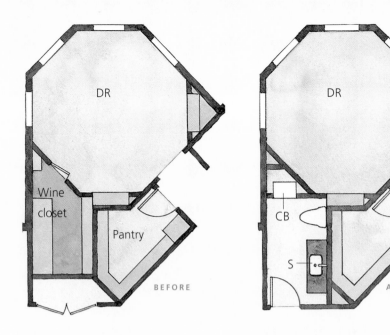

Floor plans: By closing off the door to the wine closet and creating a new door to the hallway, the architect reclaimed the space for a nicely proportioned powder room. In the new plan, the storage cabinet fits into the triangular space nestled against the octagonal dining room.

▲Before

As a walk-in wine closet just off the dining room, the space was underutilized. What the homeowners really needed was a small powder room handy to a side entrance used by family and visitors.

▼ **Cabinets built into the far wall** have the same durable finish as the vanity. Polished-chrome bar pulls and knobs establish a pleasing pattern on the doors and drawers.

After ▶

Both posh and practical, this **DAPPER POWDER ROOM** makes a positive impression on guests and is convenient for family members as they dash in from outdoors. The cantilevered, wall-mounted vanity features a high-gloss, sprayed-on finish; high-sheen vinyl wallpaper is impervious to water. For a shot of darker color, the designer framed the mirror as a piece of art.

◄ *Verde chaine* **granite from Morocco** injects bold color and pattern into the subdued palette; the white trough sink acts as a pure-and-simple foil for the highly figured countertop.

▲ Before

Serviceable but woefully out-of-date, the existing bath needed rethinking to make it suitable and appealing to young children. Tile wainscoting was a feature worth repeating, but prim wallpaper was not.

Fresh surfaces, basic After ▶

shapes, and primary colors add up to a **CLEAN AND SIMPLE** bath for kids. White subway tiles—lowered to a child's height around the sink and toilet—serve as a plain backdrop for a blue-and-red tile border. In tribute to the home's early-20th-century character, the design incorporates a new casement window, a mirrored medicine cabinet, and period-style sconces.

Floor plans: The existing layout, common in homes of the era, featured two doors into the bathroom. Eliminating one door created wall space for a chest of drawers, as well as room to shift the sink and toilet. Though slightly smaller, the new plan is more efficient.

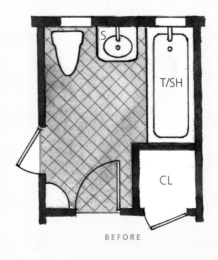

BEFORE

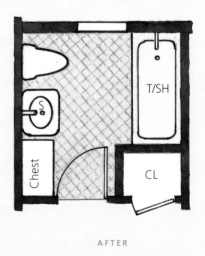

AFTER

◄ **The new pedestal sink** and wide-spread faucet with ceramic levers only *look* old-fashioned; rounded corners on the sink make it safer for kids.

▲ **For interest underfoot,** a double border of blue punctuates the white ceramic hexagonal floor tiles.

◄ **Tub-shower fittings** include a bar-mounted, hand-held sprayer with an extended hose, a practical fixture for bathing small children.

A powder room off the entry lacked the comfort and drama the homeowners desired. Large-scale wallpaper and poorly placed light fixtures didn't suit the room's tall, narrow proportions.

Before ▼

▼ **The gleaming vessel sink** is composed of copper over stainless steel; a wall-mounted faucet with brushed-nickel finish operates by a single lever.

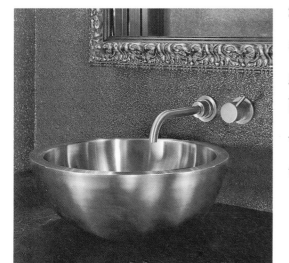

After ▲

Glass-beaded wallpaper the color of copper transforms the small room into a **SUMPTUOUS SPACE.** Crystal sconces and a mirror with a "softening" finish flatter guests. The black, crackle-finish vanity began as a desk; careful placement of the vessel sink kept the working drawers. A taffeta curtain screens the relocated toilet.

▲ A type of freestanding tub, a custom-built stainless steel *furo* (a Japanese-style soaking tub) sits on a bed of stones at the edge of the master bath, contributing a sculptural element to the room.

Tub Styles

Home improvement centers and bathroom showrooms overflow with tub styles and options. Take a quick look at your choices.

Recessed Tubs

Still the most popular model, the space-saving recessed tub is designed to fit between two side walls and a back wall. You see only the apron on the face of the tub; tile (or other wall covering) extends over the tub flange. Standard recessed tubs are 60 inches long and 14 inches deep, but they come as long as 72 inches and as deep as 16 inches.

Drop-in Tubs

Designed for platform or sunken installations, drop-in tubs may be self-rimming (with a lip that overlaps the tub deck) or undermounted for a sleeker look and easier cleaning. Only the inside of the tub is finished; the sides are not visible. Drop-in tubs are available in a multitude of styles and configurations.

Corner Tubs

These tubs come in different shapes but are always installed with two unfinished sides fitted into a corner, against adjoining walls. On a triangular (or otherwise angled) corner tub, the front is finished; a basic rectangular corner tub has one finished side and one finished end.

Freestanding Tubs

The old-fashioned claw-foot is the quintessential free-standing tub, but streamlined versions designed to sit inside a frame or rest on the floor are increasingly popular in contemporary baths. All sides are visible and finished on a freestanding tub.

Whirlpool Tubs

Think of this model as a deep bathtub with a pump and hydromassage jets. Most units resemble standard drop-in tubs, although you'll find claw-foot tubs with whirlpool features. Jet options vary, from high pressure and low volume (a few strong jets) to low pressure and high volume (many softer jets).

◀ A corner tub with angled apron makes it easy for the kids to hop in and out of the whirlpool bath. Ceramic tiles on the walls can take lots of suds and splashes.

▼ Calcutta white marble on the tub deck and backsplash accentuates the clean, classic lines of this undermounted drop-in tub.

▲ Spare and elegant, this freestanding tub offers a minimalist take on a traditional claw-foot style. A swath of pebble flooring demarcates the tub area yet blends beautifully with the warm-toned bamboo flooring.

▶ A raised-panel apron dresses up the face of this recessed tub. On the surrounding walls, the tiles extend to the edges of the tub, covering the flange.

93

▲ Before | Much more than

a remodel of one small bath, this ambitious project included a significant addition to the site and the reconfiguring of the master suite. Nothing in the old bath was to be retained.

With combined | After ▶

restraint and precision, the architect employed a simple palette of materials to create a master bath steeped in **JAPANESQUE STYLE.** Horizontal cedar paneling encircling the room establishes order and tranquility, while limestone and ceramic tiles lend color, pattern, and texture to other surfaces in the space.

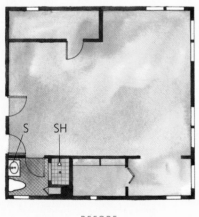

BEFORE

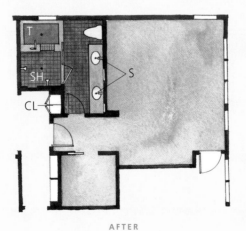

AFTER

Floor plans: The compact plan has a dual-sink vanity, deep tub, spacious shower, and toilet. Running the shower and tub together— only a low wall divides them—capitalized on the space and married the task of getting clean with the therapy of a long, hot soak.

▲ **In a fusion of disparate materials,** 4- and 2-inch ceramic tiles cover the shower walls and tub interior in soothing color. Wrapping the lower walls are 12-inch limestone tiles; darker Portuguese limestone caps the tub and trims the walls.

▶ **For a window near the property line,** the architect chose laminated glass— grass paper sealed between two pieces of plain glass— which blurs the view just enough to protect privacy.

▶ **The vanity** is a lesson in pleasing repetition: Frameless cabinets with full-overlay doors and drawers echo the rectilinear lines of the paneling; the slab limestone on the countertop reappears as 2-inch-wide liner pieces below the mirror.

▲ **Pull-out drawers** keep items stowed in the base cabinet organized and accessible. Visible are the Euro-style hinges used in combination with full-overlay doors; see "Vanity Basics," pages 64–65.

▶ **The sloped-back soaking tub** measures 2½ by 4½ feet, with a depth of 28 inches. In a nod to Japanese minimalism, the "overflow" is an integral part of the design: Water runs over the tub threshold and onto the shower floor, like a waterfall.

◀ **Before** | Garish finishes and a cultured-marble countertop gave away this master bath's age, but the lack of a tub was its biggest defect in the eyes of the homeowners.

▼ **After** | Reminiscent of an era when baths possessed a timeless beauty, the new, expansive space exudes an air of **QUIET CLASSICISM.** White millwork contributes a strong architectural element; matching mirrors over the vanity and tub reflect the sumptuous materials. For the counter-top and the generous tub surround, the architect selected Calcutta marble, which is a bit warmer than pure-white Carrara.

▶ **Intended to echo the past**—when unfitted furniture was the norm in baths—the footed cabinet makes a modern move, transitioning smoothly to the tub deck.

▶ **Satin-nickel faucets** with lever handles adorn the European-style vanity. A narrow wood bead around each door creates a shadow line and just a hint of depth.

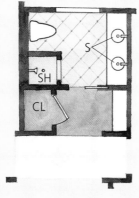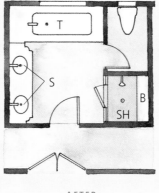

Floor plans: To attain a more open plan that would include a tub, the architect eliminated the dressing table and closet from the existing space. In the new bath, a larger shower, with a bench, was another goal achieved.

◄ **Before** | Glass block enclosing the shower and screening the toilet overwhelmed the existing bath and accentuated its unusual proportions. The homeowners hoped to turn the space into a restful retreat, complete with soaking tub and dressing table.

◀ After | Porcelain

tile walls carry the materials palette from the floor upward, blending convergent planes while making the most of the room's **STRIKING GEOMETRY.** "We're both fond of things Japanese," say the homeowners, "but we wanted to stop short of pure, stark minimalism." Working closely with their architect, they researched materials and fine-tuned their preferences to achieve their own aesthetic.

▶ **A desire for a shower** without a door led to a half-wall that shields the dressing table from splashes. The small window opens to release steam and reveal a lovely waterfront view.

Bathroom continues ▶ ▶

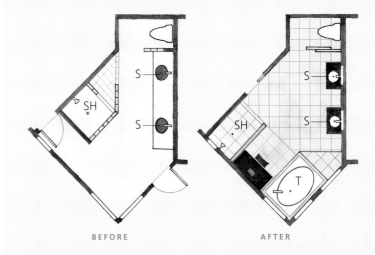

BEFORE   AFTER

Floor plans: The J-shaped room was a good example of a bad layout: the shower enclosure ate up square footage and was an unpleasant visual barrier to the rest of the room. In the new plan, the shower, dressing table, and tub occupy previously wasted space, leaving the center of the room open.

NOTES FROM THE ARCHITECT

"Windows added to the tub wall allow light to spill into the central area, while the small shower window brightens that end of the room. It's all about bringing light into a room, then spreading it throughout the space."

LESSONS FROM THE HOMEOWNER

*"The porcelain tile used throughout was probably the biggest challenge in the entire project.
Take the time you need to plan the layout—and be there while the tile is being installed.
No matter how skilled your installer is, once it's cut, it's cut."*

102 STRIKING GEOMETRY

◀ **One of the homeowners** had a big hand in the remodel, designing the privacy shoji screen and adapting a pair of bedside tables to accept vessel sinks and gooseneck faucets. What appear to be surface-mounted mirrors are, in fact, two recessed medicine cabinets, also designed and fabricated by the homeowner.

▶ **Unable to find a dressing table,** the homeowners purchased a desk at an outlet store and simply cut 6 inches off the back. They added basket drawers found elsewhere. Fluorescent fixtures light the angled mirror.

▼ **An electric towel warmer** with chrome finish keeps towels toasty and convenient to the tub.

◀ **The gooseneck tub filler** and hand-held sprayer supply a bit of sparkle in a room with mostly matte finishes; lever handles control the water temperature and flow.

▲ **Inches were everything** when it came to the high-arc, single-lever faucets: they had to fit gracefully between the vitreous china vessel sinks and the mirrored cabinet doors.

Floor plans: The long vanity with dual sinks in the existing bath made the room feel more like a corridor than a welcoming retreat. With a shortened vanity, the toilet now fits easily at the end of the cabinet run, and a shower occupies the space where the toilet once stood.

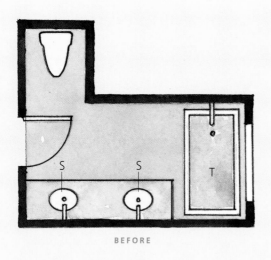

BEFORE

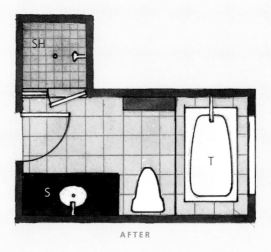

AFTER

▲ Before | To stay within budget on a whole-house remodel, the homeowner and designer opted to upgrade the guest bath without enlarging its footprint. A sunken tub was a "must go" feature, but the absence of a shower was the biggest drawback.

Outfitted in rugged slate | After ▶ and other earthy materials, the new bath has a decidedly **NATURAL BENT.** A wall-mounted vanity with slatted lower shelf and under-cabinet lighting exposes more of the floor for an expansive effect. Glossy black granite and bronze drawer pulls complete the cherrywood cabinetry.

◀ **For a slightly smoother surface**—and a dash of color—the designer chose 3-inch tumbled-marble tiles for the shower floor; 1-inch tiles of the same stone make up the mosaic trim strip.

◀ **A raised soaking tub** under the garden
window provides a peaceful place to bathe;
for ventilation and fresh air, the window
slides open. The mahogany storage piece
holds bath extras while adding sheen to
the mostly matte palette.

▲ In this master bath, the shower glass, partially sandblasted for privacy, admits natural light and enhances the open feel.

▼ With a set of doors separating the tub and toilet from the dressing area, two can comfortably use this bath at the same time. Frosted-glass panels preserve privacy yet permit the exchange of light.

Privacy Matters

We ask a lot of our bathrooms, and no demand is more personal than the desire for privacy. In the interest of providing that sense of comfort and security, designers and architects have compartmentalized bathrooms, setting the toilet apart from the rest of the room or shielding it with a visual barrier.

Take a look at four common approaches to enhancing privacy:

■ A remodel offers the best opportunity to create a separate space for the toilet. A compartment with a door affords the greatest sense of solitude and allows the bath to be used by more than one person at a time. To conserve space, many toilet compartments feature a pocket door. Obscuring glass in the door can keep the small room from feeling claustrophobic.

■ For a slightly more open look, consider a toilet alcove with a full or partial wall that blocks the view. An upper opening in a floor-to-ceiling wall will admit light into the alcove and provides a sense of cohesion.

■ A toilet partition or screen is effective when a dividing wall is not an option. The partition may be made of any obscuring material; satin-etched glass and frosted acrylic panels are among the most popular choices.

■ Layout can also promote privacy: Simply placing the toilet at the end of the vanity, away from the door, makes it feel more protected.

▼ Obscuring glass in the pocket door of this combined toilet and shower compartment (the shower is directly opposite the toilet) allows light to enter but blurs the interior.

▲ Translucent shoji-screen inserts provide complete privacy in a small toilet compartment next to a shower. Traditionally made of rice paper, shoji screens today are usually fabricated from fiberglass and other synthetic materials treated to look like rice paper.

◀ In an ultracontemporary bath, a frosted-glass screen shields the toilet without detracting from the metropolitan aesthetic.

▶ An etched-glass pocket door with decorative detailing closes off a toilet/tub compartment from the shower area in a handsome master bath.

▲ Before | Fussy wallpaper, dark

wood furniture, and a dull vinyl floor made this diminutive bath seem even smaller. The toilet and sink were ready for replacement, but the budget didn't allow for moving the plumbing.

Outfitted in sparkling surfaces, | ## After ▶

tailored components, and breezy colors, the new bath is **POSITIVELY SHIPSHAPE.** Beadboard paneling with cap and base molding gives the room much-needed "bones." A pedestal sink replaces the vanity and directs attention to the checkerboard tile floor. With beadboard on either side—and a fresh coat of matching paint—the original half-door to the attic all but disappears.

Bathroom continues ▶ ▶

◀ **Chrome hardware** on the tilt mirror, sconces, and glass shelf gleams against a backdrop of blue and white. A wide-spread faucet with old-fashioned lever handles completes the sink in vintage style.

▶ **To mask a serviceable** but unattractive sliding door, the homeowner hung a cotton-duck shower curtain from a wire "rod."

▲ **The horizontal lines** of a traditional wood shutter with 3½-inch louvers make a narrow window appear larger.

▶ **A yellow-and-white glazed bookcase** assumes a new role as a freestanding cupboard; flat curtain panels tied to wood pegs conceal items stored on lower shelves.

Before | An ordinary layout, boring vanity, and harsh light bar left a lot to be desired, but the real problem with the existing bath was its location. It was time to rethink both the bath and the adjoining master bedroom.

With its bold blend of traditional | **After** ▶

European styling and modern application of timeless materials, the new master bath proves that good design can indeed be **SET IN STONE.** Together, the homeowners and designer planned the broken-edge granite backsplash to complement the octagonal window. For privacy, the window is fitted with glue-chip glass.

▼ **Four-inch-deep shelves** set between the studs supply storage near the end of the tub. At left, a tiered towel bar with rack contributes a sleek, shiny touch.

▶ **The refinement carries over** into the shower, where chrome fixtures sparkle against porcelain tiles made to look like honed marble. Cherrywood cabinetry stained the color of cabernet provides a deep-toned base for the green-flecked granite countertop.

112

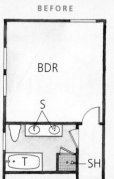

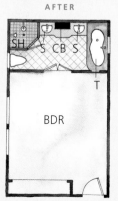

BEFORE

AFTER

BDR

S

T

SH

SH   S CB S

T

BDR

Floor plans: In the existing plan, the bath was sandwiched between two bedrooms—but served neither one well. Taking out a wall, shortening the hall, and "flipping" the bath and master bedroom areas made room for a spacious, secluded master suite. (The other bedroom became a home office.)

▼Before

"It was a sad layout," lamented the designer, "a large but poorly organized space." The homeowners, a couple with young children, were willing to give up the tub for a shower where they could easily bathe the kids.

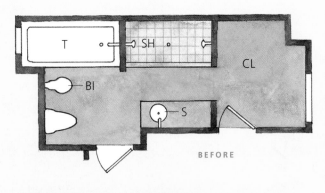

BEFORE

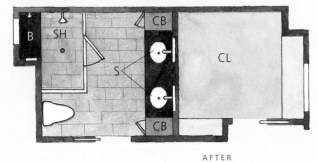

AFTER

Floor plans: The existing plan had a glaring flaw—the door to the bath interfered with the door to the master suite. In the new layout, a pocket door solved that problem, and a more compact bath layout left enough room for a larger, separate walk-in closet.

Pietra grigia slate atop the vanity,

After ▶

⅝-inch glass tiles blanketing the backsplash wall, and black slate tiles on the floor establish a calm, cohesive mood in this **TAILORED MASTER BATH.** Deep, floor-to-ceiling storage cabinets made of maple stand, like bookends, at either end of the vanity. *Bathroom continues ▶▶*

◀ **Frameless cabinets with full-overlay doors** and drawers (see pages 64–65) work well with the minimalist scheme. When the doors close, the Euro-style hinges disappear completely.

▶ **A shower bench** topped with *pietra grigia* slate fits into what was once the tub alcove. Satin-nickel fixtures include a thermal-balance system and a hand-held sprayer tucked into the corner. A window, large by shower standards, vents moisture and admits light.

▲ **A removable hamper** resting on tracks in the base of one storage cabinet keeps used towels and laundry off the floor.

▶ **Medicine cabinets** flanking the fixed center mirror open by means of small pulls at the lower corners. Milky-white ribbed-glass shades on pendant lights illuminate the vanity.

Color Palette

Light, medium, and dark hues have their place in this quiet scheme. Gray-green glass tiles read as nearly neutral on the vanity, backsplash, and shower walls. Working downward, medium-gray slate on the countertop and shower bench looks weightier, while chalky black slate on the floor grounds the room.

Situated next to the family **Before ▶** room (and near an exterior door to the pool), this small powder room saw plenty of foot traffic. More storage for pool towels and accessories was just one of the makeover goals.

Guests and family now **After ▶** "run in from the pool" to a **STYLISH AND EFFICIENT** new bath. Shifting the toilet to the exterior wall made way for a room-length vanity with a counter-to-ceiling storage unit. Clear maple cabinets and a solid-surface countertop match materials used in the nearby kitchen.

◀ **An interior window** in place of the original door lets light into the hallway while preserving privacy in the bath. The laminated glass is made of rice paper sandwiched between two layers of clear glass.

Floor plans: With the door now located on the wall shared with the family room, swimmers can more easily access the powder room. The move also eliminated that horror of horrors—a clear view of the bath from the dining room.

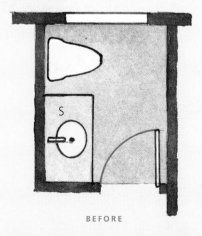

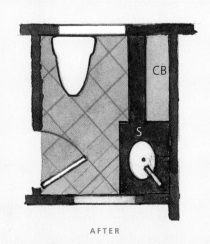

BEFORE

AFTER

Satin-etched glass (a newer version of frosted glass) in the upper cabinets masks the contents.

A mirrored backplate on the light bar creates the illusion of a floating fixture.

A stainless steel bar-sink faucet features a spout that swivels and a pullout sprayer tip, both handy in a bathroom frequented by kids.

A combination of 1-inch mosaic glass and 8-inch porcelain tiles protects the walls.

Universal Design

Remodeling a bath provides the perfect opportunity to apply the safety and accessibility features known collectively as Universal Design, or UD. Simply put, Universal Design is *good design* because it considers the needs of everyone, no matter what their physical abilities are.

The bath plans on these pages—a master bath and a hall bath—illustrate common design issues and workable solutions. For the hall bath, which originally doubled as a guest and kids' bath, there are two plan options; each borrows from a large adjacent bedroom to create separate spaces for guests and the children.

In addition to the many UD features noted on the floor plans, you might want to include the following:

- Handles, pulls, and knobs that can be operated with one closed hand or a wrist

- Contrasting materials that act as a visual cue to a change in elevation, such as a shower threshold

- Variable lighting that can go brighter when a vision-impaired person enters the space; controls and electrical outlets placed at a comfortable height

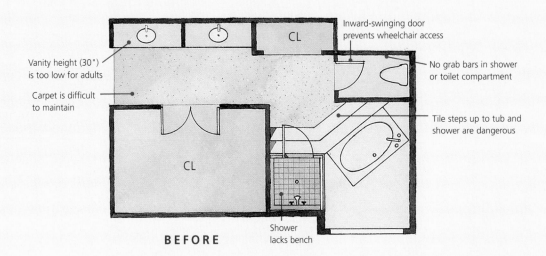

Vanity height (30") is too low for adults

Carpet is difficult to maintain

Inward-swinging door prevents wheelchair access

No grab bars in shower or toilet compartment

Tile steps up to tub and shower are dangerous

CL

CL

Shower lacks bench

BEFORE

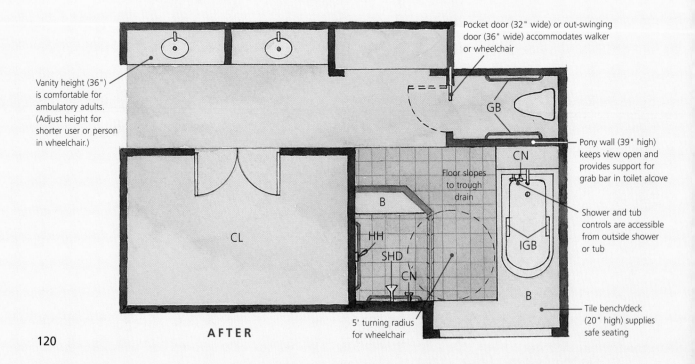

Pocket door (32" wide) or out-swinging door (36" wide) accommodates walker or wheelchair

Vanity height (36") is comfortable for ambulatory adults. (Adjust height for shorter user or person in wheelchair.)

Pony wall (39" high) keeps view open and provides support for grab bar in toilet alcove

Shower and tub controls are accessible from outside shower or tub

Floor slopes to trough drain

GB

CN

CL

B

HH

SHD

CN

IGB

B

Tile bench/deck (20" high) supplies safe seating

5' turning radius for wheelchair

AFTER

Narrow space between tub and
vanity is difficult to keep clean

Difficult to access
tub/shower control
while standing
outside tub

CN

CL

Inadequate
storage

2' door is
too narrow

BEFORE

DESIGN TIP

If grab bars are not
installed at the time
of your remodel, ask
the contractor to
brace the walls for
future installation.

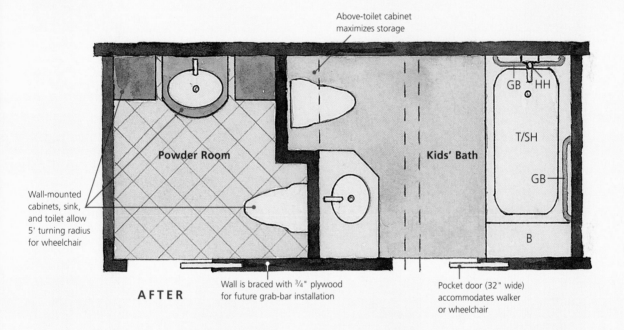

Above-toilet cabinet
maximizes storage

GB   HH

T/SH

GB

B

Powder Room

Kids' Bath

Wall-mounted
cabinets, sink,
and toilet allow
5' turning radius
for wheelchair

AFTER

Wall is braced with ¾" plywood
for future grab-bar installation

Pocket door (32" wide)
accommodates walker
or wheelchair

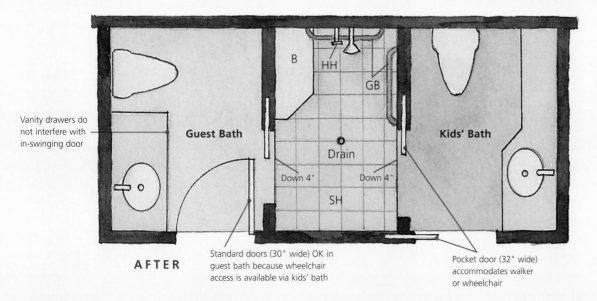

B   HH

GB

Guest Bath

Drain

Down 4"   Down 4"

SH

Kids' Bath

Vanity drawers do
not interfere with
in-swinging door

AFTER

Standard doors (30" wide) OK in
guest bath because wheelchair
access is available via kids' bath

Pocket door (32" wide)
accommodates walker
or wheelchair

▲ **Before** | Converted from a home into office space in the 1960s, a stately Victorian was ready for a return to its original purpose. The owners began the ambitious remodel with the powder room, the first of three new baths.

Using glass, wood, **After** ▶ stone, and metal, the architect took the building back to its roots as a residence—this time in **CLEAN-LINED, CONTEMPORARY STYLE.** In the new powder room, a vitreous china vessel sink stands on a faux-finished pedestal. Stainless steel liner tiles and 8-inch ceramic tiles form the wainscoting.

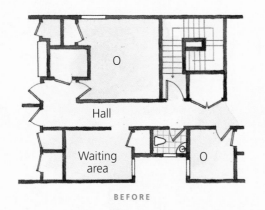

BEFORE

AFTER

Floor plans: What was once an office is now "her" bath; "his" bath occupies the former waiting area. The powder room location stayed the same.

An elongated sconce is composed of polished chrome, metal mesh, and frosted glass.

Textured wallpaper is another neutral element in the low-key color scheme.

Interior doors throughout the home feature horizontal divisions; satin-etched glass in this pocket door makes reference to the liner-tile pattern.

▲ **Venetian green marble** on the shower walls and floor befits a masculine bath. The clear maple vanity and the elevated glass sink and counter balance the darker stone surfaces.

▶ **In her bath,** a full-length vanity with a lowered makeup station and mirror was designed to accommodate the existing window above. *Arcobaleno* granite topping the stained-ash cabinetry inspired the color palette; on the floor, a combination of purple glass and tumbled-marble tiles sets a syncopated pattern. The tall niche, reflected in the mirror, adds to the elegance.

Before

A small bath off the master bedroom benefited from a sunny exposure but lacked a sense of style.

▼ **Limestone tiles** make reference to the sink backsplash; a 3-inch border of marble tiles separates the patterns of larger tiles.

Tradition takes a contemporary turn in the renewed bath, with a modern application of **TIME-HONORED MATERIALS.** Oak trim, honed limestone, and Venetian plaster establish a warm, masculine palette. Behind the sink, 1-inch polished-marble tiles in chocolate brown accent 12-inch limestone tiles set in a quarter-turn pattern.

After ▲

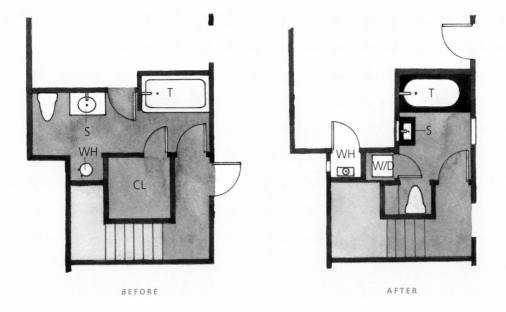

BEFORE   AFTER

Floor plans: Locating the toilet in an alcove, where a closet once was, leaves the central area of the bath open. The room is actually smaller by a bit yet feels more spacious.

▲ Before | Carved out of an existing bedroom,

this narrow bath had an inefficient floor plan, with the tub, sink, and toilet located on the same side of the room. Two doors—one to the bedroom, one to a hall—limited privacy; what was left of the bedroom felt like a rectangular box.

China black slate on the vanity and mirror sill introduces another kind of slate to the materials palette.

▼ **A stacked washer/dryer** is strategically located yet out of sight when the door is closed. The mirror reflects the door to the hall; the translucent glass admits needed light into the room.

From two unimaginative | **After** ▶

rooms emerge a **RESTFUL, RESTORATIVE BATH** and a better-proportioned bedroom. To achieve the impression of a larger space, the architect specified a console vanity with slatted lower shelf. The generous tub, encased in Brazilian green slate, makes clear that this is a *bath* room.

The recessed mirror has a trompe-l'oeil effect, appearing to be an opening in a "landlocked" room without any exterior windows.

For a staggered, masonry-like pattern, 18-inch sandstone tiles were cut into 3-inch strips and set in a random horizontal pattern.

NOTES FROM THE ARCHITECT

The homeowner chose to retain and refinish the original fir flooring.
"It had lots of character," says the architect, "which others might see as blemishes.
This house has a history, and the floor tells the tale of its use."

▲ Before | A small

bath in this Eichler-designed tract home "was hardly a master bath," the designer said. The goal? More space and light.

"This is our private | After ▶

beach," the ocean-loving homeowner says, "a relaxing environment that's as much 'retreat' as it is 'bathroom.'" Beams painted cool green accentuate the **MID-CENTURY MODERN** character of the home. A wall-mounted electric towel warmer just outside the shower is a nod to the new.

Floor plans: The new space was significant: An 8-foot addition placed the entire bathroom against what was the exterior wall. An energy-efficient, on-demand water heater is contained within thick walls, behind closet doors.

BEFORE

AFTER

LESSONS FROM THE HOMEOWNER

"If you make a beautiful bathroom, don't plan to enjoy it alone! Everyone's toothbrush is in here now—the kids don't even use their own bathroom."

130 MID-CENTURY MODERN

◀ **Fixed mirrors** on either side of a center medicine cabinet deliver a near-seamless reflective surface across the width of the vanity. Frameless cabinets with full-overlay doors and drawers are cherry-wood; wall-mounted faucets with a satin-nickel finish feature single-lever controls.

▶ **A wall-mounted body jet** just to the right of the shower niche targets the back when a person is standing, the neck and shoulders when seated.

▲ **One-inch mosaic glass tiles** on the apron and shower walls are a mix of polished and "beach-glass" (matte) finishes.

▶ **The solid surface** on the tub deck, vanity countertop, and shower bench is a resin-and-quartz composite. The homeowners chose this material for its ease of cleaning, stonelike appearance, and—most of all—durability.

▲ Dual self-rimming sinks add to the masculine mini-malism in this master bath. Because the homeowner is tall, the sinks are on 36-inch kitchen cabinets rather than standard 31-inch units.

Sink Selections

Welcome to a new generation of bathroom sinks. No longer limited to the standard white basin for washing hands and brushing teeth, today's styles are anything but mundane.

Deck-mounted Sinks

While a basin attached to a vanity is still the most common sink setup, the mounting method is now the defining feature:

A self-rimming sink overlaps the countertop to form its own edge. Inexpensive and simple to install, this sink tends to collect grime, however, where the rim meets the counter.

An undermount sink is installed from below. This style is pricier but, with no countertop edging, it's sleeker and easier to maintain.

In the realm of above-counter models, the freestanding or recessed vessel sink is most popular; less common is a high-sided, rectangular trough sink.

Integral Sinks

A sink that has been fabricated as part of the countertop has no seams or joints, so installation and cleaning are a snap. These sinks are usually made from a solid-surface material; concrete is one of several alternatives. Integral sinks withstand heavy use but are somewhat expensive.

Pedestal Sinks

Available in both traditional and contemporary designs, pedestal sinks are ideal for powder rooms or other baths where space is at a premium. These elegant towers consist of the basin and the column, or pedestal; they are typically made of vitreous china.

Wall-mounted Sinks

Think about an inexpensive, compact, wall-hung sink for a small bath or kids' bath, where clutter is common. For wheelchair access, this style is by far the best choice.

Console Sinks

If you like the design of a pedestal sink but long for a bit more counter space, consider a console sink. This model combines a rectangular deck with two or four furniture-like legs; the space below may be open or fitted with shelves.

◄ An undermount sink made of vitreous china provides a crisp counterpoint to a figured granite countertop—and an uninter-rupted, easy-to-clean surface.

▲ A pedestal sink complements the classic lines of frame-and-panel doors in a formal bath.

▲ An integral sink fabricated as part of a concrete counter takes center stage in this spa bath. The matching backsplash houses a wall-mounted faucet.

▶ In an all-white bath, console sinks and chrome wide-spread faucets look clean and crisp. Slim chrome legs support the sinks, while rack shelves below can stow extra towels or bath supplies.

▼ Wall-mounted sinks with an integral countertop offer an easy-to-clean setup in this twins' bath. To bring in a bit of color and texture, the homeowners chose cobalt blue accent tiles for the backsplash and a mirror framed in bamboo.

An intricately painted pedestal | # Before ▶

sink and decorative tile looked much too frilly for the new owner of this waterfront home. Contemporary forms and finishes were more in sync with his style.

Reflective surfaces and congruent shapes transform the small | # After ▶

space into a study in **MODERN GLAMOUR.** A round mirror hangs over a sea of glass tiles, while the pearwood vanity follows the curve of the sink. Subtle variations in the tile mix—lighter from the tub to the floor, slightly darker behind the vanity—intensify the illusion of light spilling across the room.

For design continuity, the front plane of the vanity slips behind the glass and continues as the face of the tub-shower ledge.

◀ **Fluorescent light fixtures** flanking the mirror skim the countertop for a streamlined look. A special "skin" on the shades diffuses the light.

Inconsistencies in the edges and surfaces of the glass tiles maximize the shimmer.

Honed limestone on the countertop acts as a matte foil for the glistening tiles.

A wall-mounted faucet eliminates visual clutter from the countertop; the pop-up drain control is installed in the stone surface.

...th with a **Before** ▶

...r combination and stock ceramic tile was functional, but the home-owners longed for a walk-in shower and a scheme anchored in natural stone.

Tumbled-marble **After** ▶ tile covers the vanity and lines the shower, **SETTING A WARM, EARTHY TONE.** The homeowners did most of the projects themselves, on a strict budget, to allow for one splurge—a frameless shower door.

◀ **With assistance from a contractor,** plumber, and tile installer at different stages of the project, the homeowners set the shower tile and installed a glass-block window.

◀ **Stripes painted off-white and taupe,** then dabbed with pearl-toned glaze, give the walls a soft patina. Glass shelving rests on corner pieces intended for crown molding.

Mosaic trim pieces on the vanity backsplash are a combination of ceramic tile and tumbled marble.

A brushed-nickel finish on the center-set faucets is in smooth, shiny contrast to the matte-textured stone.

▲Before

A spacious exercise room with two bay windows was the raw material from which the architect fashioned a compartmented bath. More than half of the original room was to remain dedicated to fitness equipment.

After ▶

At once soothing and exhilarating, this **MODERN, MULTI-TASKING BATH** is a lesson in polished and appropriate design. To promote an accessible atmosphere—the bath is located off the pool—no closed cabinetry or concealed storage exists. For a sense of unity, slab limestone benches and glass tile surfaces continue from one compartment to another.

Exercise room

BEFORE

S

B

B

Exercise room

B SH

AFTER

Floor plans: Pocket doors close off compartments for privacy when several people use the bath, then open to create one free-flowing space for a solitary bather.

138

▲ **In the toilet room,** a white vessel sink rests on a countertop of *crema Europa* limestone. Matte-finish glass tiles form the backdrop for the single-lever, wall-mounted faucet; above, a slim mirror and torch sconces reflect and augment the natural light.

▶ **Limestone mosaic tiles** arranged in a fan motif introduce a curvilinear pattern to the rectilinear rooms, while taupe grout picks up the hues in the benches.

▼ **For storage,** the changing room includes warm wood shelves the same thickness as the limestone benches; polished-chrome robe hooks hold pool towels and swimsuits. (The pocket-door hardware is visible in the jambs.)

Color Palette

Sandy-toned limestone and pale green glass tiles balance warm and cool color; off-white limestone acts as a neutral. The designer chose to juxtapose finishes as well: Glossy white walls are in crisp counter-point to the matte-finish tiles and honed limestone. Plush towels in persimmon serve as a hot accent.

◄ **To suggest a more open shower** in a windowless, confined space, the lime-stone benches and wall tiles appear to slip through the glass partition. Details make the difference: Narrow trim tiles that begin atop the backsplash in the toilet room (see facing page) continue through the changing room and into the shower.

Design and Photography Credits

DESIGN

6–7 Peter Brock (principal), Marina Rubina (project architect), Peter Brock Architect, www.peter-brock.com; 8–9 Christel Heinelt and Thaddeus Warren, Lushart Decorative Painting & Murals, www.lushart.com; 10–12 Peter Soldat, Peter Soldat Architecture, www.soldatarch.com; 13 Architect: Anne Laird-Blanton Designs, www.alb designs.com; 16–19 Fox Design Group, Architects, www.foxdesigngroup.com; 20T Design: Heidi M. Emmett; 20B Design: Melinda D. Douros and D. Kimberly Smith, Deer Creek Design; 21TL Architect: John Lum; 21TR Interior Design: Amoroso Holman Design Group; 21BL Design: Debra S. Weiss; 21BR Interior design: Carolyn E. Oliver-Broder, Oliver's Interiors and Antiques, www.oliversinteriors.com; 22–23 Philip Volkmann, Barry & Volkmann Architects, www.bvarchitects.com; 24–26 Architect: Chase, Diengott Architecture; 27 Design and construction: Harrell Remodeling Design + Build; interior design: Genie Nowicki, www.harrell-remodeling.com; 28–33 David S. Gast & Associates, Architects, www.gast architects.com; interior design: Kathy Geissler Best, KGB Associates; construction: Plath & Co., Inc.; lighting: Anna Victoria Koldoff; 34T Interior design: Philip J. Meyer Ltd., www.philipjmeyerltd.com; 35L Design: Annette M. Starkey, CKD, CBD, Living Environment Design; 35BR Tish Key Interior Design, www.tishkey.com; 36–37 Design: Christine E. Barnes; 38–39 Interior design: Kimberly Ayres Interior Design and Lawanna Cathleen Endonino Design; 40–43 Architect: Arnold Mammarella; Marcy Voyevod Interior Design, www.marcyvoyevod.com; construction: Eron Ersch; tile: Cairo Cocalis, Zoo Gang Studios/Flying Spark Furniture, www.flying sparkfurniture.com; 44–47 Architect: Kathryn A. Rogers, Sogno Design Group, www. sognogdesigngroup.com; 48–49 Design: Annette M. Starkey, CKD, CBD, Living Environment Design; construction: Dale Nichols, Artisan Remodeling; 50T Architect: Kathryn A. Rogers, Sogno Design Group, www.sognogdesigngroup.com; 50BL Katherine North, Northbrook Design, www. northbrookdesign.com; 51TL and TR Design: Annette M. Starkey, CKD, CBD, Living Environment Design; 50BL Architect: Kathryn A. Rogers, Sogno Design Group, www. sognogdesigngroup.com; 50BR Architect: Halperin & Christ; interior design: Sharon Low; contractor: Cam Fraser; 52–54 Marcy Voyevod Interior Design, www.marcy voyevod.com; cabinets: Kit Young, East Bay Cabinets, www.eastbaycabinets.com; 55 Interior design: Jay Jeffers, Jeffers Design Group, www.jeffersdesigngroup.com; 56–59 Design: Melinda D. Douros and D. Kimberly Smith, Deer Creek Design; 60–63 Architect: Reynolds Gualco Architecture-Interior Design,

www.rgaid.com; interior design: Robin Hardy Design; construction: Thomas Irvin; 64T Louie Leu Architect, Inc., www.louieleuarch.com; interior design: Ann Sheerer; Komo Construction, Inc., www.komoconstruction.com; 64BL Graff Architects; 64BR Design: Vasken Guiragossian; 65TL and TR Interior design: Danielle Schneeloch, www.danielledesigns. com; 65B Interior design, Jeanese Rowell Design, www.jrdesign.com; 66–70 Peter Brock (principal), Marina Rubina (project architect), Peter Brock Architect, www.peter-brock.com; 71 Tish Key Interior Design, www.tishkey.com; 72–73 Design: Heidi M. Emmett and Debra S. Weiss; 74–75 Architect: Kathryn A. Rogers, Sogno Design Group, www.sognogdesigngroup.com; 76–79 Design: Annette M. Starkey, CKD, CBD, Living Environment Design; 80 Prototype Architecture, www.prototypepdx.com; 81TL Gary Earl Parsons, Architect, www. garyearlparsons.com; 81TR Design: Fired Earth, www.firedearth.com; 81BL Michael Harris Architecture, www.mbh-arch.com; 81BR William Hefner Architecture and Interiors, www.williamhefner.com; 82–84 Architect: E. Paul Kelly; Marcy Voyevod Interior Design, www.marcyvoyevod.com; cabinets: RK Designs; McCutcheon Construction, Inc., www.mcbuild.com; 85 Design: Zach Rosen; 86–87 David S. Gast & Associates, Architects, www.gastarchitects. com; interior design: Kathy Geissler Best, KGB Associates; construction: Plath & Co., Inc.; lighting: Anna Victoria Koldoff; 88–90 David S. Gast & Associates, Architects, www.gastarchitects.com; construction: D.V. Rasmussen & Son; 91 Interior design: Ashley Roi Jenkins Design, wwwarjdesign.com; 92T Spears Architects, www.spearsarchitects.com; interior design: Stephen Watkins Design; 92B Philip Volkmann, Barry & Volkmann Architects, www.bvarchitects.com; 93L Louie Leu Architect, Inc., www.louieleuarch.com; interior design: Ann Sheerer; construction: Komo Construction, Inc., www.komoconstruction. com; 93BR Interior design: Danielle Schneeloch, www.danielledesigns.com; 94–97 David S. Gast & Associates, Architects, www.gastarchitects.com; construction: D.V. Rasmussen & Son; 98–99 Hamid R. Hekmat, HRH Architecture, www.hrharchitecture.com; interior design: Beverly Stowell; Podesta Construction, Inc., www.podestaconstruction. com; 100–103 Fox Design Group, Architects, www.foxdesigngroup.com; 104–105 Interior design: Janice Stone Thomas, CKD, Stone-Wood Design, Inc., www.stonewooddesign. com; 106T Michael Mullin Architect, Ltd., www.michaelmullin.com; 106BR Kanner Architects; 107TR Philip Volkmann, Barry & Volkmann Architects, www.bvarchitects. com; 108–111 Design: Debra S. Weiss and D. Kimberly Smith, Deer Creek Design; 112–113 Owner/builder: Paul and Bobbi

Maniscalco; interior design: Liza Moloney, Focal Point Kitchens; 114–117 Interior design: Navarra Design, Inc., www.navarra design.com; 118–119 Design and construction: Harrell Remodeling Design + Build; Interior design: Lisa Sten, www.harrell-remodeling.com; 120–121 Design: Annette M. Starkey, CKD, CBD, Living Environment Design; 122–124 Architect: Anne Laird-Blanton Designs, www.albdesigns.com; 125 Interior design: Katherine North, Northbrook Design, www.northbrookdesign.com; 126–127 Peter Brock (principal), Marina Rubina (project architect), Peter Brock Architect, www.peter-brock.com; 128–131 Architect: Arnold Mammarella; Marcy Voyevod Interior Design, www.marcy voyevod.com, construction: Eron Ersch; lighting: Marcie Shefren; 133B Philip Volkmann, Barry & Volkmann Architects, www.bv architects.com; 133TL Interior design: Nahemow Rivera Group, www.nahemow riveragroup.com; 133TR Interior design: Danielle Schneeloch, www.danielledesigns. com; 133BL Philip Volkmann, Barry & Volkmann Architects, www.bvarchitects.com; 133BR Weston & Hewitson, Architects; 134–135 Jerry Veverka and Johanna Forman, Veverka Architects, www.veverka.com; 136–137 Design: Heidi M. Emmett and Debra S. Weiss; 138–141 David S. Gast & Associates, Architects, www.gastarchitects. com; interior design: Kathy Geissler Best, KGB Associates; construction: Plath & Co., Inc.; lighting: Anna Victoria Koldoff

PHOTOGRAPHY

Before, 98T: **Matt Podesta**
After: *If not otherwise credited, photographs are by* **Margot Hartford.**
Dave Adams: 35L, 48–49T, 49B, 51TL, TR, 61–63, 77–79, 104, 105; **Stephen Fridge:** 98B, 99; **John Granen:** 106BL; **Ken Gutmaker:** 27B, 118L, 119; **Jamie Hadley:** 8B, 9, 34T, 38B, 39, 51BR, 64BR; **Muffy Kibbey:** 11, 12, 22BL and BR, 23, 25, 26, 41–43, 53, 54, 64BL, 81TL, 83, 84, 92B, 106T, 107TR, 129–131, 132B, 133BL; **david duncanlivingston:** 34B, 35TR, 50BL, 65TL, TR, 91B, 93BR, 107BR, 133TR; **E. Andrew McKinney:** 20, 21TR, 21BL and BR, 36BL, BR, 37, 50BR, 56–59, 65B, 72, 73, 108–111, 136L, B, 137; **Matthew Millman:** 55B; **Daniel Nadelbach:** 107L; **John O'Hagan:** 14L, 14BR, 15, 132T; **Heather Reid:** 74B, 75; **Rusty Reniers:** 8T, 38T, 91TL, 125TL, 133TL; **Ken Rice:** 91TR, 125TR, B; **Sharon Risedorph:** 21TL, 64T, 93L, 123, 124, 134B, 135; **Lisa Romerein:** 92T; **Susan Seubert:** 80; **Thomas J. Story:** 81BL, 85B; **Tim Street-Porter:** 106BR; **Mark Trousdale:** 13B; **Brian Vanden Brink:** 93TR, 133BR; **Dominique Vorillon:** 81BR

Index

Index (cont.)